Early Missouri Marriages in the News

1820-1853

by

Lois Stanley

George F. Wilson

Maryhelen Wilson

Please direct all correspondence and orders to:

www.southernhistoricalpress.com
or
SOUTHERN HISTORICAL PRESS, Inc.
PO BOX 1267
375 West Broad Street
Greenville, SC   29601
southernhistoricalpress@gmail.com

ISBN #0-89308-437-9

Printed in the United States of America

Since the publication of our first two volumes of Missouri marriages in newspaper records (1851 and later) we have received a number of requests for similar records from earlier periods.

The result is this compilation, of approximately 800 marriages from 49 Missouri newspapers. Most of these records give the name of the bride's father (or a widowed mother); others include such details as former residences, location of the ceremony, etc.

A separate, and important, category are records of women marrying as "Mrs." This notation appears infrequently in civil records, yet it may be a vital clue in genealogical research.

Some of these records are reports of Missourians marrying outside of the state, which appeared in newspapers not available at the time we published our "Missing Marriages" collection; and a few, from the same newspapers, report marriages in "burned" counties.

Generally, these marriages occurred in the 1830s and 1840s, with a few in the 1820s and in the 1850-51 period (one or two 1853 reports slipped in). The two earliest were in widely separate areas, for one was in Howard Co. in February 1820 and the other in Cape Girardeau Co. in June of the same year. The newspapers searched covered 16 counties, but most reported from a wider area.

Newspaper codes are on the following page; most of them are available in the Newspaper Library of the State Historical Society of Missouri, in Columbia; a few are in the library of the Missouri Historical Society in St. Louis.

The Brides' Index starts on page 47.

Code		Location
BEA	Beacon	St. Louis, St. Louis Co.
BGDB	Democrat-Banner	Bowling Green, Pike C .
BGRAD	Radical	"
BOBS	Observer	Boonville, Cooper Co.
BORE	Register	"
BOLT	Boonslick Times	Fayette, Howard Co.
BRUNS	Brunswicker	Brunswick, Chariton Co.
CANE	Northeast Missourian	Canton, Lewis Co.
COGL	Globe	Columbia, Boone Co.
COP	Patriot	"
COMB	Commercial Bulletin	Boonville, Cooper Co.
CGWE	Western Eagle	Cape Girardeau, Cape Gir. Co.
FAME	Farmers' and Mechanics' Advocate	St. Louis, St. Louis Co.
FREEP	Free Press	"
HAG	Gazette	Hannibal, Marion Co.
HAJ	Journal	"
HANJ	"	"
HWU	Western Union	"
INP	Independent Patriot	Jackson, Cape Girardeau Co.
JASO	Southern Advocate	"
JEFRE	Republican	Jefferson City, Cole Co.
JEM	Metropolitan	"
J-MOH	Missouri Herald	"
LADB	Democrat-Banner	Louisiana, Pike Co.
LEXA	Appeal	Lexington, Lafayette Co.
LEXP	Express	"
MIN	Missouri Intelligencer	Published first in Franklin, then Fayette, then Columbia
MOAR	Argus	St. Louis, St. Louis Co.
MOP	Reporter	"
MORE	Republican	"
MOSN	Saturday News	"
MODE	Missouri Democrat	Fayette, Howard Co.
MOH	Missouri Herald	Jackson, Cape Girardeau Co.
NERA	New Era	St. Louis, St. Louis Co.
PAMC	Missouri Courier	Palmyra, Marion Co.
PAMJ	Marion Journal	"
PWH	Whig	"
PLAR	Argus	Weston, Platte Co.
SASE	Sentinel	Savannah, Andrew Co.
SJA	Adventure	St. Joseph, Buchanan Co.
STGAZ	Gazette	"
SLDU	Daily Union	St. Louis, St. Louis Co.
SLINT	Intelligencer	"
SLNL	News Letter	"
SLOB	Observer	"
SWERE	Weekly Reveille	"
SPRIG	Whig	Springfield, Greene Co.
SRJ	Salt River Journal	Bowling Green, Pike Co.
WARV	Visitor	Warsaw, Benton Co.
WEM	Western Emigrant	Boonville, Cooper Co.

ACHLIE, Charles F. in Cooper Co. 14 June   COMB 20 Jun 1846
MACK, Ellen Jane (Squire N. M.)   Rev. A. D. Corbin

ADAMS, James E.   in Franklin Co. 8 March   MORE 15 Jun 1849
NORTH, Mary E.   at the home of William North
                   all of Franklin Co.

ADAMS, Maj. T. M. of New York City 21 October   SWERE 8 Nov 1847
BUCKNER, Anna W. (Benjamin)   Rev. James Inskeep
               at Prospect Hill in Jackson Co.

ADDERTON, Marcus L.   3 June   MORE 12 Jun 1834
RULAND, Matilda Ann (Isaac)   Rev. Ball
                   all of Troy, Lincoln Co.

ADERTON, A. J. of Arrow Rock   in Saline Co. 13 Feb.   MORE 20 Feb 1845
VENABLE, Amelia (Dr. H. S.)   Rev. Hickman

ADKISSON, William of Saline Co. in Cooper Co. 8 June   COMB 10 Jun 1847
ALLISON, Selinda (Thomas, of Cooper Co.) Rev. P. G. Rea

ALEXANDER, Spencer   in Livingston Co. 27 July   JEM 17 Aug 1847
JOHNSTON, Mrs. Catherine   Rev. Wm. T. Ellington

ALFORD, J. N.   in Herculaneum "recently"   MORE 15 May 1832
LEWIS, Mrs. Adaline (Elias Bates)

ALLEN, Col. F. J. of Jackson   24 Nov   CGWE 29 Nov 1850
HILL, Eliza Ann (Samuel A.) of Cape Girardeau
                   by Rev. Nelson Henry

ALLEN, Robert M. of Front Royal, VA   in Boone Co.   COMB 5 Nov 1846
ALLEN, Mary (Elder T. M.) 26 November Rev. T. N. Gaines

ALLEN, Maj. Shubael of Clay Co.   in Howard Co.   MIN 24 Sep 1822
TRIGG, Diana (Gen. Stephen)   "Thursday last"
                   by Rev. Edward Turner

AMENT, Joseph A., editor of the Hannibal Courier   BRUNS 5 May 1849
RUFF, Sarah Jane of Augusta Co. VA 12 April in Palmyra

AMSBURY, M. P.   in Johnson Co. 24 December 1844   LEXP 21 Jan 1845
BRADLEY, Mary Ann (James & Lucy)   Rev. James Porter

ANDERSON, Larz   2 March, no minister or JP shown BRUNS 17 Mar 1849
HERYFORD, Missouri (Charles, of Keytesville)

APPLETON, George D. of St. Louis   in St. Louis   MORE 7 Mar 1850
HOUGH, Kate (George, deceased) late of Alexandria VA
               5 March by Rev. W. G. Eliot

ARNOLD, Harvey of Monroe Co.   30 August   MORE 20 Sep 1837
HILL, Nancy Jane of Bourbon Co. KY
                   by Rev. Benjamin Davis

ARROT, James, formerly of Philadelphia 25 January   MORE 4 Feb 1844
BERRY, Ann (Col. Isaac deceased) no minister shown
                   in Franklin Co.

AUSTIN, Archibald   in Carroll Co., no date shown NERA 13 Jan 1846
AUSTIN, Lucy J. (2nd daughter of Ezekiel, of Spencer Co. KY)
                   by Rev. Henry Renick

1

BACON, Dr. T. M., formerly of Liberty   10 August   SJA 23 Aug 1850
MAHONY, Frances Ann (Maj. L.) of Liberty
          by Rev. Z. N. Roberts

BAKER, Thomas F.   in Osage Co. 18 May   JEM 30 May 1848
GOODMAN, Polly (Robert)   Judge C. Leay

BAKER, Hampton of Monroe Co. in Marion Co., in January PWH 6 Feb 1841
SHROPSHIRE, Susan (Jeremiah)   Rev. Fuqua
        His name appears as "Baber" in records.

BAKER, Capt. W. W.   18 September MORE 23 Sep 1849
WOOLFORK, Mary M. (eldest dau/Isaiah) Rev. James Fleming

BALEY, Samuel Green of Chariton Co.   18 November   MODE 1 Dec-
WRIGHT, Frances (William) of Howard Co.   29 Nov 1847
         no minister or J.P. shown

BALLARD, T. J.   in Jefferson City   JEFRE 26 Mar 1836
HODGE, Mary (Josiah) of KY   Rev. H. H. Baber

BARADA, Andrew   in St. Louis 25 October   MORE 27 Oct 1849
PHILIBERT, Eliza (Joseph Sr.)
     Probably a Catholic wedding, but no priest shown.

BARADA, Richard (P. D.) 8 November in Carondelet MORE 12 Nov 1849
POURCILY, Angelique   Rev. Ortleb

BARBEE, Elias W.   in Marion Co. 15 June   PWH 17 Jun 1843
TERRELL, Amanda (Robert, of Union Twp.) Rev. Broaddus
      His name appears as "Owen" in records.

BARBER, William M.   in St. Louis 11 November   MORE 13 Nov 1849
CRANE, Mrs. Sarah Sophronia
       "by the Law Commissioner of St. Louis"

BARCLAY, R. M. of St. Louis in St. Charles Co. 13 June NERA 18 Jun 1849
LANGHAM, Wenona (Maj. E. J., of St. Louis)
         by Rev. Mayhew

BARNARD, George, of St. Louis near Louisiana, Pike Co. MORE 21 Jul 1840
JACKSON, Attilla   16 July by Rev. W. McQuie
        at the home of J. C. Jackson

BARRETT, Dr. J. Addison   in St. Louis 18 July   NERA 19 Jul 1849
MOORE, Helen M. (Dr. John S.)   Rev. Potts

BARTLETT, Sanders H.   in Pike Co. 3 August   LADB 14 Aug 1848
MARIAR, Mrs. Nancy   John Massie, J.P.
        all of Louisiana, MO

BARTLEY, George   in Callaway Co. 29 August   JEM 14 Sep 1847
MOORE, Margaret Jane (Wharton) no minister or JP shown

BARTON, Abraham in Jefferson Twp., Cole Co.   JEFRE 4 Oct 1834
ASKINS, Harriet (Dennis)   Benjamin M. Lisle, JP
        all of Cole Co.

BARTON, John M. of St. Louis in Dover 5 September MORE 14 Sep 1847
POWELL, Artemesia E. (Rev. M.) Rev. Willis Mathew

BASCOM, Hiram B.   12 January?   Rev. Tabor   MOAR 13 Jan 1837
HENSEY, Catherine Jane (Benjamin) late of Lynchburg VA

BASYE, Dr. Alfred "Wednesday evening last"   JEFRE 11 Apr 1835
WALKER, Hellen (John, State Treasurer of Missouri)
                by Hon. George Tompkins

BATES, Henry of Herculaneum   in Potosi 17 December   MORE 29 Dec 1829
MARTIN, Mary (William) of Potosi   Rev. Donald

BATES, John F.   in St. Louis 21 May   MORE 24 May 1853
ELLIOTT, Mrs. M. A.   Rev. W. G. Eliot
          Record shows her as Mary Ann Thomas.

BATES, Maj. Stephen   10 December in Pulaski Co.   JEM 1 Jan 1850
COWAN, Mary Ann (Col. Wm. Bowie Cowan)   Rev. Hovey

BATTE, Benjamin B.   in St. Louis 4 February   SLDU 8 Feb 1847
SHURLDS, Josephine (Henry)   Rev. William Potts
               all of St. Louis Co.

BEARDSLEY, Charles S. of St. Louis (son of William   MORE 3 Oct 1844
            Beardslee & Frances Freeman)
SMITH, Hannah Andromache of Cape Girardeau (daughter
            of Robert Smith & Ann Walker)
       in Cape Girardeau 26 September by Rev. Megary

BELL, Andrew J. of St. Louis   14 April   MORE 23 Apr 1846
SMOOT, Damarus A. (Middleton) of Lewis Co.
                by Rev. Tyson Dines

BELL, David   26 September in Franklin Co.   MORE 9 Oct 1839
CAMPBELL, Nancy K. (James L.)   Rev. James K. Rule

BELL, Dr. J. T. of Lincoln Co. in Bowling Green   MORE 29 Sep 1841
OURY, Elizabeth (Maj. Augustus) 21 September
                by Rev. Campbell

BELL, Dr. Robert H. in Benton Co. 25 November   JEM 1 Dec 1846
FERGUSON, Sarah (R.)   Rev. I. W. K. Handy

BELLES, Caleb   26 December 1844   LEXP 7 Jan 1845
WARDER, Mrs. Abigal   of Lafayette Co.
            no minister or J.P. shown

BENNING, I. F.   24 June   LADB 4 Jul 1846
JORDAN, Sarah (Andrew)   Rev. Hedges
                all of Pike Co.

BENSON, James L. of Hannibal   in Marion Co.   PWH 21 Nov 1840
BLAKEY, Lucinda Ann (Maj. William of Palmyra)
            by Rev. Tucker Tuesday evening last

BENT, Col. John, attorney of St. Louis in Boone Co.   MORE 29 Sep 1829
McCLELLAND, Olivia L. (Col. James)   Woods, J.P. no date

BENTLY, Jordan   in Howard Co.   no date   JEM 1 Dec 1846
FRISTOE, Susan Martha (eldest dau/Rev. T.)
                by Rev. Lewis

3

BERCIER, Benjamin   11 February   CGWE 16 Feb 1849
GILES, Alice   W. S. Watson, J. P.)
                "at the home of John Taylor near Cape Girardeau"

BERRY, Taylor H.   in Waterloo, Clark Co., 8 October   MORE 16 Oct 1844
HARMON, Caroline T. "at the home of Dr. Lurton"

BERRY, Willis G. of Ste, Genevieve in Jefferson Co.   MORE 13 Jan 1840
HART, Mrs. Sarah (James McCormack)
                24 December 1839 by Rev. W. G. Walker

BIGGER, Hiram L. of Ralls Co.   29 February   PWH 16 Mar 1844
HARRISON, Mary Eliza of Calhoun Co. IL   Rev. Allen Gallaher

BIOREN, C. B. of New Orleans 20 Jul at Monticello   BOLT 24 Jul 1841
LEWIS, Mary Frances (S. W.) Rev. Hommans of Jefferson City
                (Monticello is in Howard Co.)

BIRCH, Thomas Erskine   19 May in Howard Co.   BOLT 22 May 1841
MORROW, Eliza G. (Capt. Christopher)   Rev. Boon

BLACK, Leazer   in Troy, Lincoln Co. no date   MORE 14 Jun 1839
PARKER, Lucretia M. (F.)   Rev. McElroy

BLACKBURN, Henry   16 November   JEM 30 Nov 1847
FOSTER, Mrs. Rhoda Ann of St. Louis Co.
                Record shows him as William H.

BLACKLEDGE, Hiram in Ste. Genevieve 22 October   MORE 19 Nov 1846
SMITH, Mrs. Mildred (Col. Coffman)
                "at the home of Col. Joseph Coffmann"

BLAIN, Albert of Potosi   in Farmington 15 June   MORE 24 Jun 1843
SIMS, Mary (Nancy) of St. Francois Co. Rev. Covington

BLAKEY, Maj. John Clark in Marion Co. 24 February   PWH 26 Feb 1842
HUNTSBERRY, Mary Ann Amanda (Abraham) Rev. Lanius

BLEDSOE, Milton   in Marion Co. 19 September   PWH 23 Sep
SHANNON, Laura (Mrs. Malinda)   Rev. N. Parks   1843

BLOCK, Hyman (Phineas)   19 September   MORE 25 Sep 1848
SOUTH, Lucy (Gen. John, of Bowling Green) Rev. Davis

BLOCK, Jacob   12 November in Louisiana MO   MORE 18 Nov 1843
ADAMS, Catherine (Levin)   no minister or J.P. shown
                "at the home of Levin Adams"

BLOCK, William Henry 15 May in Troy, Lincoln Co.   NERA 21 May 1845
WOOLFOLK, Mary J. (John A.)   Rev. T. I. Wright

BOGGS, James C.   "last Sunday in Franklin"   MIN 29 Jan 1830
GAW, Barbara Ann (John, deceased)
                no minister or J. P. shown

BOHANNON, Robert R.   Thursday   BOLT 16 Jan 1841
HEADRICK, Mary (Jacob) "all of this city"
                by Isaac B. House, J. P.

BOSWORTH, Col. Lorin   Tuesday last   BRUNS 23 Dec 1848
PRICE, Kate (Ransom) "all of Brunswick"
                no minister or J. P. shown

4

BOTTS, Seth Esq. in his 70th year   31 March   MODE 14 &
LITTREL, Elizabeth in her 30th year   12 Apr 1847
                    Presumably in Howard Co.?

BOWERS, Dr. George H. 16 November   BRUNS 25 Nov 1848
PORTER, Mary Haseltine (eldest dau/Rev. William H.)
              "all of Chariton Co. ," no minister shown

BOWLBY, James H. of St. Louis 20 September   SLDU 26 Sep 1846
MORGAN, Mary L. (Joel) of Philadelphia
              by Rev. Charles Woolsey

BOWMAN, Charles E. of Richmond, Ray Co. 18 June   LEXP 24 Jun 1845
EWING, Pamela M. (Col. T. M. of Lafayette Co.)
              by Rev. Yantis

BRACKEN, Andrew J. of Louisiana, Pike Co. 3 March   MORE 9 Mar 1846
SIMONDS, Jane (Oliver) in Troy, Lincoln Co.
              by Rev. Thomas Wright

BRACY, John of Vicksburg MS 9 October   LADB 14 Oct 1850
PUGH, Joanna (Joseph) of Pike Co. Rev. Walter McQuie

BRADFORD, Dr. C. M. of Saline Co. in Howard Co.   BOLT 30 Oct 1841
PEARSON, Lavinia   by H. L. Boon, Tuesday
          "at the home of C. F. Jackson near Fayette"

BRADLEY, James   15 February   BOLT 27 Feb 1841
GIBSON, Zerelda Ann (Martin) Rev. Thomas Fristoe

BRANT, Capt. Joshua B., USA   Thursday last   BEA 2 Jan 1830
BENTON, Sarah (Samuel, of West Tennessee) Rev. Potts
          "at the home of Hon. Thomas H. Benton"

BREDELL, Edward, an attorney   6 April   FAME 11 Apr 1835
PERRY, Angeline Cornelia (Samuel) late of Washington Co.,
              MO.   by Rev. Jenney

BRIDGES, Thomas   12 September in Jackson Co.   MORE 30 Sep 1839
CORN, Nancy (Martha) no minister or J.P. shown

BRIGGS, F. B.   27 May by Michael Hatton, J. P.   COP 11 Jun 1842
DALEY, Sarah (J. W.) "all of Boone Co."

BROADWATER, John S. 14 September in Callaway Co.   JEM 28 Sep 1847
TRIMBLE, Margaret (Mrs. Ann) no minister or J. P. shown

BROWN, Henry M. of St. Louis   2 May   MOSN 5 May 1838
WILLIAMS, Martha Ann (Olly) of St. Louis Co.
              by Justice McKenney

BROWN, John Henry   in Ashley, Pike Co.   MORE 25 Jul 1843
MITCHELL, Mary, of Connecticut Dr. Pharr, no date shown

BROWN, John J. "Thursday evening last"   CANE 8 Nov 1849
LEAMAN, Eliza J. (Rev. C. A.)   Rev. E. M. Marvin
              "all of Tully"

BROWN, Robert T. Jr. 22 January in Perry Co.   MORE 1 Feb 1838
HOLDEN, Mary Elizabeth (Col. E. M.)   Rev. Raho

BROWN, William M., late of Jefferson Co. NY   PLAR 29 Dec 1848
EVERETT, Susan J. of Jackson Co. MO 7 December
           "at Newmarket, Platte Co."

BROWNLEE, John A. of St. Louis in Baltimore 27 July   NERA 2 Aug 1845
RIDGLEY, Hannah (Noah)   Rev. Thomas Atkinson

BRUCE, Capt. Amos   4 January   BEA 13 Jan 1830
DAVIDSON, Rebecca (George of Belleview Twp., Washington Co.)
           by Rev. Thomas Donald

BRUCE, Col. Amos G.   12 December in Washington Co. MORE 24 Dec 1839
LeCLAIRE, Theresa M. (Louis)   Rev. Tuckey

BRUNS, Frederick E. of New York City 28 August   CGWE 30 Aug 1850
LEWIS, Mrs. Virginia of Cape Girardeau
        by Rev. George W. Bushey, Methodist

BRUNS, Dr. H. Walker   "Wednesday week" in Howard Co. BRUNS 30 Dec 1847
LEWIS, Sarah Jane (Judge Henry) no minister shown

BRYAN, John Gano   in Washington Co. 6 November   MORE 20 Dec 1827
McILVAINE, Evaline (John)   Rev. Thomas Donnel

BUCHANAN, Arguyle M.   20 April   FAME 24 Apr 1834
LEWIS, Viena (L.)   Rev. R. Rennick
         "all of St. Louis Co."

BUCKNER, A. H., Editor of the <u>Salt River Journal</u>   PWH 25 Sep 1841
MINOR, Mrs. Eliza L. (Maj. James Clark) of Lincoln Co.
       16 September, no minister or J. P. shown

BULLARD, Coleman   28 July   JEM 17 Aug 1847
BOWEN, Fanny (Andrew)   Elder Jacob Coons

BULLARD, James M., a merchant of Greenton 16 February COP 3 Mar 1842
WALTON, Elizabeth M. (James), late of Sumner Co. TN
       in Lafayette Co. by Rev. Robert Sloan

BUNDRIDGE, John   2 March   BOLT 13 Mar 1841
RICHARDSON, Delilah (Elijah)   H. L. Boon
        "all of this county"

BURCH, Dr. Benjamin F. in Osage Co. 14 March   BRUNS 31 Mar 1849
       (he of Linn Co.)
McDANIELL, Frances E. (John) of Osage Co.
      no minister or J. P. shown

BURNES, James Nelson in Platte Co. 15 July   MORE 29 Jul 1847
SKINNER, Mary A. (Phineas) Rev. J. Wilson, Methodist Church
       "all of Platte Co."

BURNS, Peter Jr., merchant of St. Louis 7 April   NERA 21 Apr 1845
BURGESS, Mary T. (John D.) of Mason Co. KY
      by Rev. Ebenezer Rogers

BUTLER, Andrew Jackson of Marion City, in Marion Co. PWH 25 Jan 1840
CLIFFORD, Mrs. Joanna L. of Palmyra
      by Rev. W. P. Cochran

BYNUM, Stephen   "Thursday last"   BRUNS 30 Mar 1848
MALLORY, Frances W. (William T.) no minister shown
                "all of Fayette"

BYRAM, Augustine   in Jackson Co. 8 November   JEM 23 Nov 1847
GRAY, Mrs. Elizabeth   no minister or J. P. shown

CAKE, Francis   15 May in Troy   NERA 21 May 1845
WOOLFOLK, Rebecca A. (John A.) Rev. T. I. Wright

CALLIHAN, Dr. Stuart   27 April   JEFRE 5 May 1838
NEWMAN, Henrietta S. (Michael) Rev. Robert H. Jourdin

CAMERON, Capt. N.   1 December   HAG 5 Dec 1846
MATSON, Fanny (Enoch)   Rev. B. B. Bonham
                "all of Ralls Co."

CAMPBELL, Andrew   in Boone Co. 8 August   JEM 17 Aug 1847
JONES, Mrs. Margaret J.   Rev. Roberts

CAMPBELL, George   in Madison Co., no date shown   MORE 10 Nov 1829
STONE, Mary Ann (eldest dau/Micajah)
                no minister or J. P. shown

CAMPBELL, Capt. John   16 June   PWH 25 Jun 1842
MALONE, Mrs. Mary   William G. Wilson, J. P.

CAMPBELL, Dr. John A.   "Wednesday week" in Keytesville BRUNS 14 Jun 1849
McNAIR, Mary (Elizabeth) of Fayette
                no minister or J. P. shown

CAMPBELL, Rev. Thomas   21 October   MIN 29 Oct 1822
PAUL, Mrs. Pembroke   Rev. Tharp

CANNON, John M.   no date shown   SLDU 27 Aug 1847
FARLEY, Mrs. Ann M. F.   Rev. Berryman
           "all of St. Louis; Mobile and Montgomery, AL
                        please copy"

CANOLE, Charles   18 April in Howard Co.   MODE 5 &
McKINNEY, Mrs. Nancy of Warren Co.   3 May 1847
           "near Marthasville;" no minister or J.P. shown

CARLISLE, Capt. John   3 September   NERA 5 Sep 1845
WILLIAMS, Frances A. (William P. of Hyde Park, NY)
                by Rev. Hugh Boyle

CARR, Levi T. of St. Joseph, MO   21 October   NERA 24 Oct 1845
BLOCK, Eliza Ann (E. M., of St. Louis) Rev. Potts

CARSON, Robert   in Howard Co. 19 March   MIN 27 Mar 1829
CALLAWAY, Harriet (Charles) Nicholas Burckhartt, J.P.

CARTER, E. E. in Richmond, Ray Co., 19 December   BRUNS 30 Dec 1848
SCOTT, Mrs. Jane (Edward Camplin) of Boone Co.
                no minister or J. P. shown

CARTER, John N. of Woodford Co., KY in Franklin Co.   MORE 8 Jul 1844
BAKER, Eliza J. (Martin, deceased) of Louisa Co. VA
                2 July by Rev. Thompson

7

CARY, David S.   28 March   LADB 3 Apr 1848
ORR, Mrs. Martha E.   John Massie, J.P.
            "all of Buffalo Twp., Pike Co."

CASH, Samuel   Tuesday, 28 March, in Howard Co.   MIN 7 Apr 1826
OLIVER, Nancy (William)   John Harvey, J.P.

CAVE, Benjamin of Boone Co.   in Howard Co.   MIN 9 Jul 1825
TURNER, Jane of Howard Co.   Eb. Rodgers
            "at the home of James Turner"

CHADWICK, Alfred   2 April in St. Louis?   MORE 5 Apr 1850
PALMER, Elizabeth H. of Boston   Rev. W. G. Eliot

CHAFEY, John H.   "Wednesday evening last"   JEFRE 1 Jun 1844
FRASIER, Therese (John, of St. Charles Co., among the
                first settlers in that county)
            by Rev. M. D. Noland

CHAMBERLAIN, Rev. Hiram of St. Charles 16 August   MORE 19 Aug 1842
GRISWOLD, Mrs. Anna Adelia   in Pinckney, Warren Co.
            by Rev. Walker D. Shumate

CHAPELL, Henry of Grundy Co.   11 January   BRUNS 20 Jan 1849
HALL, Minerva (James C.) of Chariton Co.
            no minister or J. P. shown

CHASE, Dr. Robert P.   3 September in Boston   MORE 23 Sep 1851
RUSSELL, Elizabeth   Rev. J. Bowan Clark

CHILDS, Joshua J. of St. Louis   3 September   SLDU 7 Sep 1846
BAKER, Elizabeth of Marietta OH   Centenary Church
            by Rev. Nathaniel Childs, Jr.

CHURCH, Elder Samuel S.   5 January   JEM 9 Feb 1847
LENOIR, Julia (Walter, deceased) Elder T. M. Allen

CLANCY, John of St. Louis in Washington Co. 20 October JEM 2 Nov 1847
CASEY, Catherine (John)
        (probably a Catholic wedding, but no priest shown)

CLAPP, Edward   23 February   SLDU 26 Feb 1847
LITTLE, Ann Elizabeth (Freeman) Rev. Artemas Bullard
                "all of St. Louis"

CLARK, John B., an attorney   19 October in Howard Co. MIN 2 Nov 1826
TURNER, Ellen (Philip) no minister or J. P. shown

CLARK, John B.   5 August   NERA 8 Aug 1845
FERGUSON, Louisa (Thomas J., deceased) Rev. Potts
                "all of St. Louis Co."

CLARK, Capt. M. M., USA   26 February   MOAR 5 Mar 1840
JOHNSON, A. M. of Baltimore   Bishop Kemper

CLARK, W. E.   in Herculaneum 8 June   MORE 13 Jun 1842
ELLIS, Eliza T. (Elisha, deceased)   Rev. Lore

CLATWORTHY, John of Cooper Co.   20 April   JEM 25 Apr 1848
CLATWORTHY, Mrs. Mary   A. Fulkerson, J.P.

8

CLEGHORN, John W., formerly of Lawrence Co. NY   MORE 24 Dec 1844
HOYLE, Hannah, formerly of Manchester ENG   9 December
          in Brunswick by Rev. J. Mark Fulton
       (published record shows her name as Hayes)

CLEVELAND, John, formerly of Boston MA -- he was the Editor
               of the Missouri Intelligencer
HUGHES, Louisiana (William) of Howard Co.   MIN 12 Nov 1823
             no minister or J.P. shown

CLICK, Andrew T. C. 27 January in Marion Co.   PWH 5 Feb 1842
CORDER, Mary Virginia (Vincent) formerly of
             Rappahannock Co. VA Rev. G. D. Sumers

COALTER, Dr. Beverly T. of Clarksville 24 July   MORE 8 Aug 1834
McQUEEN, Elizabeth Jane (Judge Thomas)   Rev. Hughes
               "all of Pike Co."

COCHRAN, Rev. William T.   3 June in Howard Co.   MIN 6 Jun 1828
SCOTT, Mrs. Eliza   Rev. Thomas Durfee

COFFMAN, George   13 November in Newark, Andrew Co. SASE 22 Nov 1851
HOLMES, Mrs. Caroline Scott   William Snuffin, J.P.

HOFFMAN, Henry C. of Jacksonville, Morgan Co., 14 May   JEM 28 May 1850
McCRACKEN, Charlotte Anna of Scott Co. IL
               in Scott Co., no minister or J.P. shown

COLE, William F.   15 September in Potosi   MORE 19 Sep 1839
JAMISON, Elizabeth Jane (eldest dau/Isaac)
            By Rev. George Smith of St. Louis

COLGAN, Harvey (or Harry) N.   28 August   MORE 13 Sep 1831
FRAZIER, Mrs. Kezia (Capt. N. Simonds) in Jefferson City

COMFORT, James H.   23 October   MORE 24 Oct 1849
BACON, Mariette (Edwin, deceased) Rev. J. H. Lorance

CONWAY, F. R. of St. Louis in Washington Co., no date FREEP 23 May 1833
SMITH, Mrs. Susan Caroline   Rev. Philip Borgna

COOK, Henry, of Cook & Martin, merchants in Palmyra   PAMC 21 Nov 1835
MILLAN, Ellen (Thomas) of Palmyra   17 November
               By Rev. W. P. Cochran

COOK, James H., M.D., of St. Louis in Callaway Co.   MORE 24 May 1839
CALDWELL, Grizella S. (Capt. Thomas)   16 May
               By Rev. John Yantis

CORDELL, R. L. in Jefferson City 24 October   JEFRE 30 Oct 1841
HARDIMAN, Leona (John, deceased)   Rev. McAfee

COTTER, Edward   26 November   CGWE 29 Sep 1848
NEELY, Letitia C. (J., of Neely's Landing)
               By Rev. S. H. Ford

COTTING, Amos Jr.   1 June in Quincy, IL   MORE 7 Jun 1852
De La PORTE, Theodora no minister or J.P. shown

COUDY, Matthew of St. Louis in Montgomery Co. IL   SLDU 11 Sep 1848
SEWARD, Mary C. (Israel) Rev. Francis Springer

                              9

COURTENAY, Thomas S.   at Farmington, near Louisville   SLDU 31 Aug 1847
CLENDENIN, Mildred Ann (eldest dau/James, of St. Louis)
            "At the home of Austin Bray (?) 28 August (?)"
                    By Rev. Leighcock

COVINGTON, Dr. James M. of Potosi   30 October   MORE 26 Nov 1838
BAKER, Narcissa (Isaac) of St. Francois Co.
                    By Dr. John F. Cowan

COXE, Henry S., Cashier of the US Branch Bank   BEA 30 Dec 1830
FITZHUGH, Lucy Ann (Judge, decd) of Louisville KY
            23 December by Rev. Potts

CRAWFORD, Hugh of Lafayette Co. in Howard Co. 10 March   MIN ca 10 Mar
CLARK, Mrs. Susan   Rev. Rodgers   1830

CRAWFORD, Dr. J. H., late of Bairdstown (sic), KY   HAJ 3 Aug 1848
SHULSE, Susannah E. (Mark) of Ralls Co. 1 August
                    By John M. Johnson, J.P.

CREATH, Bishop Jacob Jr. of the Palmyra Christian Church   PWH 9 Apr 1842
ROGERS, Mrs. Prudence of Bowling Green   31 March
            By Rev. James Campbell, Presbyterian, at the
                    home of Judge Hunt.

CREWS, Enoch   Sunday last   MIN 1 Feb 1828
TOLSON, Sarah (William) of Howard Co. Rev. Edward Turner

CREWS, James of Randolph Co. 16 March   BRUNS 30 Mar 1848
MAUPIN, Mary (Garland D.) of Howard Co.
                    no minister or J.P. shown

CROWELL, William   25 April   MORE 27 Apr 1853
GUNN, Abby   Rev. Gunn of Keokuk, IA
                "at the home of her brother"

CUBBERLY, T. P.   1 December   SLDU 9 Dec 1846
HOYLE, Hannah (only dau/Lawrence, deceased)
                    By Rev. Parsons

CUNNINGHAM, Noble C. of Boonville   "Tuesday last"   BOLT 24 Apr 1841
SCOTT, Martha C. (William, of Howard Co.)
                    By H. L. Boon

CURD, John H.   in Callaway Co. 29 September   PWH 15 Oct 1842
FREELAND, Deborah A. (Major Joseph) of Callaway Co.
                    By Elder Thomas M. Allen

DARBY, John F., Mayor of St. Louis   in Perry Co.   MORE 26 Sep 1836
WILKINSON, Mary M. (Capt. Walter) of Perry Co.
                20 September by Rev. Raho

DAVIS, Dr. Daniel L. of Canton MO 3 September   HAJ 6 Sep 1849
BRIZENDINE, Mrs. Sarah A. of Hannibal Rev. G. C. Light

DAVIS, E. C. of St. Louis 12 October in Quincy IL   NERA 24 Oct 1845
SKINNER, Jane (of St. Louis?)   Rev. S. S. Parr

DAVIS, Reese   in Monroe Co. 24 March   NERA 9 Apr 1845
BOULWARE, Mrs. Sarah   no minister or J.P. shown

DAVIS, Vines   10 September in St. Louis   MOAR 14 Sep 1839
SMALL, Martha W. (2nd dau/Justice Small) Justice McKenney
                    "all of Collinsville IL"

DAWSON, Andrew J.   8 October   SLDU 9 Oct 1847
DUDSON, Mrs. Sarah   Elder Augustus Farnham

DAYTON, B. B. of Stl Louis 25 September in Philadelphia NERA 10 Oct 1845
JENNINGS, Mary Frances (John, deceased) of Philadelphia
                    By Bishop Potter

DEAN, Capt. Charles of the Die Vernon 19 May   LADB 23 May 1846
POTTER, Helen C. (only dau/William, of Troy, Lincoln Co.)
                    By Rev. William Barnett, in Aberdeen MO

DEAN, John of Cape Girardeau   7 January   CGWE 11 Jan 1850
ANCELL, Gabriella (William) of Scott Co.
                    By Ithamar Williams

DEARING, William   13 January in Marion Co.   PWH 15 Jan 1842
CARMAN, America (William)   Rev. Lanius

DeCAMP, James of St. Louis Co. 3 November in Hannibal   PWH 13 Nov 1841
PEAKE, Ellen (Dr. H.) no minister or J.P. shown

DeGARIS, John, of Hannibal   "Thursday last"   HAG 25 Nov 1847
WILLIS, Amanda C. (William, deceased) of Monroe Co.
                    By Elder Henry Thomas

DENNIS, Capt. E. H. of the Archer "Thursday last"   MODE 15/13
MONROE, Margaret R. (Rev. A., of Glasgow)   Dec 1847
                    No minister or J.P. shown.

DENT, Arthur   13 February in Marion Co.   PWH 20 Feb 1841
HAYDON, Rebecca (Col. Elijah)   Rev. Phillips
                    "all of this county"

DENT, George   14 October in St. Louis   JEFRE 30 Oct 1841
SHURLDS, Mary (eldest dau/Henry)   Rev. Griswold

DEVILBUS, Henry   26 March   CANE 28 Mar 1850
DURKEE, Amanthis (Lucian)   Rev. Burns
                    "all of this county" (Lewis)

DEWEY, Dr. George M.   "Wednesday week"   BRUNS 20 Apr 1848
EWING, Martha Jane (Col.) no minister or J.P. shown

DICKEY, William of Weston   Wednesday last in Glasgow   MODE 19 Jan 1848
McCOY, Anna J. (Thomas) no minister or J.P. shown

DICKSON, James of Monroe Co. in Cooper Co. 4 November   COMB 5 Nov 1846
LITTLEPAGE, Mrs. Nancy of Boonville Rev. Wm. G. Bell

DICKSON, Jesse   10 June (probably in Perry Co.)   SLOB 3 Jul 1834
PARKS, Rebecca B. (Joseph)

DILLARD, George A.   31 May   SPRIG 16 Jun 1849
GIBSON, Eliza J. (John H.)   Rev. John Dillard
                    "all of this county" (Greene)

DIMMITT, Dr. P. T. 31 January   CANE 7 Feb 1850
HENDERSON, Mrs. C. F.   Rev. E. M. Marvin
                    "all of this county" (Lewis)

11

DINWIDDIE, Dr. J. R.   13 July   MODE 22/
BARNES, Elender (Rev. James)   Rev. Paten Stephens   20 Jul 1846
                "all of Randolph Co."

DIXON, Samuel Dorrance of New Orleans 18 November   INP 27 Nov 1824
SHANNON, Eliza Maria (William) in Ste. Genevieve
                No minister or J.P. shown.

DOBBIN, James L., formerly of Belfast IRE 12 April   MORE 16 Apr 1833
SIMPSON, Mrs. Mary, widow of Joseph, late of Penrith ENG
        12 April in Franklin by Rev. Hampton Boon.

DOBBINS, Leonard   13 December in Shelby Co.   PWH 17 Dec 1842
BLACKFORD, Mary Jane (Judge)   Rev. R. Sharp

DOBYNS, James R.   31 December 1835   SLOB 7 Jan 1836
CRAFT, Sarah (Dr. J. L.)   Rev. Bewley

DOBYNS, Louis C. of Farmington, IA   19 May   HAG 20 May 1847
PATRIDGE, Charlotte of Hannibal   Rev. S. S. Parr

DOUBLEDAY, John W.   26 October in Callaway Co.   JEM 2 Nov 1847
BROADWELL, Ann Maria (William)
                No minister or J. P. shown.

DOUGLASS, Capt. John Thompson of the J. J. Hardin   COMB 15 Apr 1847
McPHERSON, Cornelia (E. B., of Boonville)   8 April
                No minister or J. P. shown.
        (MORE 23 Apr says Douglass was of St. Louis)

DOWNING, William G. 4 February in Memphis (MO?)   CANE 14 Feb 1850
JONES, Mary A. (Major)   Rev. J. Lanius

DOYAL, Samuel of Platte Co. in Clay Co. 2 March   PLAR 17 Mar 1848
OWENS, Lydia (John)   Elder S. Farmer
                "with J. B. Warfield attendant"

DRAKE, Charles D.   8 September   MOAR 11 Sep 1835
BLOW, Martha Ella Taylor (Capt. Peter, deceased)
                By Rev. W. S. Potts

DRAKE, Gershon F.   3 June in Adair Co.   PWH 15 Jul 1843
EARHART, Maria Louise (John B.)   Bryant, J. P.

DRAKE, Nicholas B. 8 October near Franklin   BOLT 17 Oct 1840
ANDERSON, Cecelia Sophia (Capt. A.K.) Rev. Isaac House
                "all of Howard Co."

DRAPER, Edward, merchant of Louisiana MO 14 June   MORE 22 Jun 1838
HOUSE, Urania Lowrey (stepdaughter of Levi Pettibone)
                By Rev. Light

DREYER, G. William   10 February   MOSN 17 Feb 1838
ULRICI, Anna (C.)   Rev. G. Wall

DuBOIS, C., formerly of Newburgh NY   23 October   NERA 25 Oct 1845
WHITEHILL, Mary J. (John) of St. Louis
                By Rev. J. B. Townsend

DuBOIS, William T. 23 July in Marion Co.   PWH 24 Jul 1844
MULDROW, Clarinda (Andrew & Charlot T.)
                By Rev. John Leighton

                        12

DUNCAN, J. M. of Jefferson City in Callaway Co.   JEFRE 21 May 1842
McAFEE, Mrs. Mary E.   Rev. R. I. McAfee
                         No date shown.

DUNCAN, John M., formerly of the Glasgow News   COMB 25 Sep 1847
DAVIS, Mrs. Jane E. of Keytesville   9 September
            At the home of George B. Dameron in Glasgow
                         by Rev. A. Monroe.

DUNCAN, Thomas Ogden   22 November in Christ Church*   BEA 24 Nov 1831
SAUNDERS, Jane Esther (2nd dau/C.)
                    By Rev. L. H. Corson   *Episcopal

DUNCAN, Dr. William C.   in Lincoln Co. 8 April   MORE 13 Apr 1847
ZIMMERMAN, Zuleima E. (Judge)   Elder Thomas Wright

DUNN, James, formerly of Fayette   in Benton Co.   MODE 19 Jan 1848
DUNN, Elizabeth (James) 30 February "all of Benton Co."
                    No minister or J. P. shown.

DUNNICA, Fountain M.   13 February   JEFRE 15 Feb 1834
HARRISON, Jane Caroline (Jason) Rev. John Longan

DUNNICA, James, of Jefferson City in Howard Co.   JEFRE 14 Mar 1835
HARDIMAN, Mrs. Nancy   Rev. H. Chamberlain
                    "Tuesday last"

DWYER, Francis of St. Louis   in Baltimore 2 October NERA 16 Oct 1845
HALBERT, Elizabeth Ann (John) of Baltimore Co. MD
                    By Rev. Johns

DYE, George, of Weston   in Clay Co. 27 December?   STGAZ 22 Nov 1845
MINTER, Helen (John, of Clay Co.) Rev. A. P. Williams

DYER, James of Lincoln Co.   11 July   LADB 23 Jul 1849
CAMP, Martha Emily (Joseph and Nancy) of Warren Co.
                    By Elder Jackman

EARL, William 31 August at St. Charles   MORE 2 Sep 1847
PERREAU, Eleanor (Helena)   Rev. Koontz
                    "Both of St. Louis."

EARLY, Peter, formerly of Rochester NY 12 December   SLDU 14 Dec 1848
SMITH, Bridget (oldest dau/Capt. Peter, of St. Louis)
                    By Rev. Hinds

EASTIN, Lucian Jr., Editor of the Jefferson Inquirer   BRUNS 31 May 1849
DALE, Sarah F. (eldest dau/Mrs. Ellen, of Rocheport)
            In Boone Co. 13 May, no minister or J.P. shown.

ECHERT, Joseph   19 March in Cape Girardeau   NERA 27 Mar 1846
CLARK, Mrs. E. W.   no minister or J.P. shown

EDDINS, William   Tuesday last   MODE 2 Dec-
PIERSON, Elizabeth   no minister or J. P. shown   30 Nov 1846
                "At the home of Maj. C. F. Jackson"

EDWARDS, Thomas L. of Saline Co. 20 May   MORE 23 May 1850
ROBERTS, Edwardana (William H., Superintendent of
                    St. Louis City Hospital)
            In St. John's Church, denomination not shown.

EHRMIN, Frederick   in Cape Girardeau 23 March   NERA 4 Apr 1845
GARRETT, Mrs. Mary   no minister or J. P. shown

EITZEN, Charles C. 23 April in Hermann   MORE 26 Apr 1844
KEHR, Jane (Jean), formerly of Philadelphia
                By Julius Leopold, SM

ELDER, James A.   12 November   NERA 15 Nov 1845
McCLURE, Ann Rebecca (James) Rev. Walker D. Shumate
                "all of Bridgeton"

ELLERY, Dr. William of Marion Co. in Hickory Grove   HAG 22 Jul 1847
LAFON, L. C. (Judge) of Lewis Co.   13 July
                By Rev. Holt

ELLIOTT, Capt. John of Lincoln Co. in Warren Co.   MORE 18 Oct 1847
BROTHERTON, Mrs. Mary Ann of Warren Co. 30 September
                By Rev. Y. Bowen

ELLIOTT, Thomas T. 26 October   BRUNS 4 Nov 1848
BUTLER, Mary A. V. (Nathaniel) no minister or J.P. shown
                "all of Chariton Co."

ELLIS, Alfred P. of Cape Girardeau   19 June   MOH 24 Jun 1820
WATERS, Fanny (Maj. Thomas W., deceased, of Tywapety)
                No minister or J. P. shown)

ELLIS, John M.   15 March   LADB 27 Mar 1848
BROWNING, Mildred (Capt. William) Rev. Thos. J. Wright

ELLISON, Jacob in Marine Settlement, IL 17 April   NERA 20 Apr 1849
WALKER, Mary Amanda, formerly of St. Albans VT
                By Rev. Darrow, at the home of L. S. Judd.

EMBREE, Joshua, of Randolph Co.   1 July   HAG 15 Jul 1847
SWINNEY, Ann Eliza (Joseph D.) of Monroe Co.
                By George W. Cunningham, J.P.

EMERRY, Thomas   "Sunday"   MORE 4 May 1852
NICHOLS, Mrs. Sarah   Rev. W. W. Woodward

EUBANK, Elias N.   no date shown   LADB 21 Dec 1846
CANNON, Caroline E. (Rev. Edward, deceased, of the
                        Virginia Conference)
        By Rev. William Barnett; "all of Prairieville MO."

EUBANK, Richard   6 June in Randolph Co.   NERA 24 Jun 1845
SCOTT, Mrs. M. J.   no minister or J. P. shown

EVANS, James, of Callaway Co. in Howard Co. 14 April   MIN 21 Apr 1826
ALLCORN, Elizabeth (James, of Howard Co.)
                By Rev. Redman

EVANS, John   30 March   COP 10 Apr 1841
FOSTER, Mrs. Mary   S. Smith, J. P.
                "all of Boone Co."

EVANS, Johnson   4 June   CGWE 16 Jun 1848
RUSSELL, Mrs. Catherine   Rev. N. B. Peterson
                "both of Cape Girardeau Co."

EVANS, R. P. Jr. of Fayette Co. KY (in Columbia County?) MORE 14 Jun 1831
SPIRES, Jane of Boone Co. 24 May no minister or J.P. shown
            (probably took place in the town of Columbia)

EWING, William   28 July   NERA 30 Jul 1849
WRIGHT, Mrs. Alta R.   Rev. Potts

FACKLER, John G. (Dr. Henry)   at Union, Franklin Co.   MORE 14 Mar 1843
RAINEY, Cornelia (Dabney) formerly of Caswell Co. NC
            26 February by Rev. Joseph Fenton.

FANT, Joseph L. 23 September in Warren Co.   MORE 7 Oct 1847
STEWARD, Ruth H. (Grief)   Rev. Joseph C. Nichols
                "in Warrenton"

FARR, Asa Jr. of St. Louis   in Boston, no date   NERA 24 Jul 1845
MILLARD, Mary F. (Samuel, of Boston) Rev. Neal

FARRELL, Joseph, formerly of New Orleans 4 October   MORE 6 Oct 1849
SAPPINGTON, Sarah Ann (Z.)   Rev. Gilbreath

FARTHING, Shelton B.   26 November   SRJ 12 Dec 1840
GLENN, Julia Ann   Rev. William Davis
                "all of Montgomery Co."

FAY, Albert   12 September   BEA 22 Sep 1831
WHITTLESEY, Mary Ann Augusta (Gen. C.) of Middleton CT
                By Rev. Potts

FEAZEL, John M. of Chariton Co.   1 November   SLOB 6 Nov 1834
BURKS, Martha Ann Elizabeth (S.) Rev. W. S. Potts

FERGUSON, William D. of Boonville   10 December   JEFRE 14 Dec 1839
LUNCY, Zerella (Richard, of Cole Co.)
                By Rev. M. D. Noland

FERRELL, William B. of Monroe (County?) 26 March   PLAR 31 Mar 1848
NOEL, Mary Ellen   (James O., of Platte Co.)
                By Charles Wells

FIFE, Robert   8 October in St. Louis   JEM 2 Nov 1847
HOPSON, Mrs. S. J. no minister or J.P. shown

FIFE, William G. (R. B.)   20 October   SLDU 24 Oct 1846
ROSS, Sarah Jane (William)   Rev. Hall

FINLEY, S. W. "late Sheriff of this city" 17 September   LADB 18 Sep 1848
HENRY, Angeline (Josiah) "all of Pike County"
                By Rev. George Smith at the Methodist Church.

FISCHER, Adam, of Pinckney, Warren Co. 27 November   MORE 5 Dec 1840
PARSONS, Frances (eldest dau/James, of Gasconade Co.)
                By Rev. Samuel Rogers, in Gasconade Co.

FITHIAN, Samuel B.   4 October   MORE 6 Oct 1849
LEITENDORFER, Emilie (youngest dau/John, deceased)
                By Bishop Kenrick

FITZPATRICK, R.   15 April   HAJ 22 Apr 1847
MORGAN, Margaret (Col. John) Rev. E. M. Marvin
                "all of Marion Co."

15

FLOURNOY, Matthew J.   11 November in Jackson Co.   JEM 23 Nov 1847
HOCKENSMITH, Anna (Dr. N. J.) no minister or J.P. shown

FORBIS, James B. of Chariton   4 May   BRUNS 18 May 1848
HURT, Mary Jane (Peyton) no minister or J.P. shown
        (A published record gives her name as Huett, but there
        were other Hurts marrying in the area.)

FOLWELL, James S.   14 January   LADB 18 Jan 1847
SMITH, Catherine (Chamness)   Rev. Rice

FORCE, D. M. of St. Louis   25 February   SJA 28 Feb 1851
BENIGHT, Mary (Thaddeus, of St. Joseph)
                        By Rev. T. S. Reeve
        (His name is spelled Forse, Forsee, etc.)

FORD, Rev. Samuel H. of St. Louis 2 September   NERA 16 Sep 1845
CLARK, Precilla A. S.   Rev. Noah Flood
        In Danville, Montgomery Co., whose records are lost.

FORTIER, P. M. of St. Louis   23 October   MORE 29 Oct 1849
JOHNSON, Eugenia Mary Josephine of St. Mary's Co. MD
                By Rev. A. Damon

FOSTER, Henry S. of Howard Co.   17 August   MIN 10 Oct 1828
WOLFSKILL, Margaret (George)   John Harvey, J.P.

FOWLER, William S., late of Goochland Co. VA 11 May   NERA 25 May 1848
MOORE, Eliza Jane (eldest dau/James Duke Moore)
                In St. Charles, by Rev. Thomas Watson.
                Richmond VA please copy.

FREEMAN, Thornton of VA   23 January in Carroll Co.   MORE 8 Feb 1840
ARNOLD, Statira (Judge)   Abbot Hancock, J.P.

FREEMAN, Dr. W. W. of Spencerburg   20 September   LADB 28 Sep 1846
MASE, Jemima (Col. Adam) of Frankford   Tate, J.P.

FULKERSON, Dr. P. P. of Andrew Co. "Tuesday"   JEM 9 May 1848
DIXON, Lydia (Levi, of Cole Co.)   Rev. Mussett

FUNK, Solomon of Hannibal   HAG 5 Dec 1846
WALEY, Jane of Adams Co. IL   Rev. H. Tucker of Quincy
                (Her name might possibly be Walsy.)

FUNK, William of St. Joseph   21 November   SJA 29 Nov 1850
FLINT, Mary (Dr. William P., of Buchanan Co.) Rev. Holmes

FUQUA, Moses, late of KY   6 February   FAME 21 Feb 1835
IRWIN, Harriet (Mrs. M.) of Louisiana MO, formerly of
                St. Louis. By Rev. Samuel Findly

FUNKHOUSER, Robert Monroe of St. Louis 8 April   HAJ 15 Apr 1847
SELMES, Sarah Jane (only dau/T. R., of Hannibal)
                By Rev. E. M. Marvin

GALLAHER, H. of St. Louis in Tremont IL 17 July   NERA 26 Jul 1845
ESCHENBURG, Jane (John, of Madison Co. IL)
                By Rev. Neil Johnson, at the Franklin Hotel

GALLATIN, J. M. Fischel   4 December in Jefferson Co.   MORE 10 Dec 1839
GEIGER, Harriet (eldest dau/John, of Jefferson Co.)
                    By Rev. Whitehead

GANO, Daniel of Hannibal   14 March in Liberty   HAJ 30 Mar 1848
PRICE, Margaret S. (Maj. John, of Clay Co.)
                    By Rev. J. M. C. Inskeep

GARDNER, James B.   in Fabius Twp., Marion Co.   PWH 6 Aug 1842
MOBERLY, Elizabeth   William Maddox, J.P.
            "At the home of Joab Moberly, who was present
                and consenting." (Name also shown as Mobley.)

GEIGER, Jacob   20 June   MORE 4 Jul 1848
DUDLEY, Martha (R. B.)   Thomas Wright, J.P.
                "All of Lincoln Co."

GEORGE, Warren of Ray Co.   10 March   BOLT 28 Mar 1840
PEYTON, Jane E. (Henry, of Howard Co.)
                    By Rev. Isaac S. House

GIBBS, John P. of Columbia in Callaway Co. 25 November   COMB 9 Dec 1847
ROTHWELL, Mary Ann (Dr. John)   Elder T. P. Stephens

GIBSON, William, formerly of Philadelphia   MORE 5 Nov 1825
DAGUET, Maria Louisa (Peter)

GIERS, J. J. of St. Louis in Murfreesboro TN 2 May   NERA 17 May 1849
GOOCH, Mary L. of Murfreesboro   Rev. J. Eaton

GILCHRIST, Porter   in Pike Co., no date shown   MORE 3 Mar 1840
DORSEY, Comfort (eldest dau/Col. Edward W.)
                No minister or J.P. shown.

GILLETT, Dr. B. of Jacksonville, IL   25 July   BEA 29 Jul 1830
COLLINS, Mrs. Elizabeth (C. Saunders, merchant of St. Louis)
                By Rev. W. S. Potts

GILLUM, James C.   21 December   LADB 1 Jan 1849
BRYANT, Martha (Edward)   Rev. Samuel Farr
                "All of Pike Co."

GIPSON, Andrew of Boonville in Howard Co. 11 November   BOLT 20 Nov 1841
BRANNIN, Ann (Capt. Richard) of Howard Co.
                By H. L. Boon

GLEASON, William Sunday last in Howard Co.   MIN 24 Jul 1824
ALSOP, Laura (Thomas, deceased) no minister or J.P. shown

GLEIM, Edgar   4 August   MOAR 14 Aug 1835
JOHNSON, Rosella (Col. J. W.)   Rev. Lutz

GOLDEN, Stephen of Linn Co.   9 September   COP 11 Sep 1841
COWDEN, Jane (James) of Boone Co. Rev. George M. Effinger

GOODWYN, Henry H. of St. Louis Co.   5 December   PWH 17 Dec 1842
DURRETT, Mary T. of Shelby Co.   in Marion Co.
            "At the home of Thomas Dobyns by Rev. S.C. McConnell."

GORDON, G. P.   Tuesday evening last   JEFRE 25 Jul 1842
BURCH, Mary Ann (Capt. William S.) Rev. Leander Ker (sic)

GORDON, Thomas B.   1 May   LEXP   6 May 1845
FULKERSON, Margaret (Frederick, deceased)
                      By Rev. B. R. Johnson

GORDON, Dr. W. B.   11 September   CGWE 15 Sep 1848
HENDERSON, Eliza M. (Mrs. Lucy)   Rev. S. H. Ford
            (She married David Rigby later - see this
                 record, which also appears here.)

GRANT, Barton W., merchant of Columbia 29 September   JEM   13 Oct 1846
BOWER, Mary J. (Dr. G. M.)   in Monroe Co.
                      By Rev John W. Ceatch

GRAVES, David A.   Tuesday, 1 April in Lafayette Co. LEXP 8 Apr 1845
LETTON, Lavina Campbell (Dr. J. W.)
                      By Elder T. N. Gaines

GRAVES, Edward P.   7 June in Howard Co.   BRUNS 21 Jun 1849
WOODS, Frances J. (Adam C.)   no minister or J.P. shown
                  "All of Howard Co."

GRAVES, John of Chariton Co. in Howard Co. 8 July   MIN   24 Jul 1824
LEWIS, Agnes W. (Henry, of Howard Co.)
                      By Rev. John Bull

GRAVES, William B.   5 May   BRUNS 5 May 1849
HALE, Eglantine (William, of Livingston Co.
                   No minister or J.P. shown.

GREEN, Ansel   14 December in Howard Co.   MODE   5 Jan 1848
MARKLAND, Nancy (Levi) no minister or J.P. shown

GREEN, James B. in Howard Co. 20 November   COMB 16 Dec 1847
EVANS, Mary (John, deceased)   Rev. William Shores

GREEN, Thomas P., editor of the Rock Spring IL Pioneer   MORE 20 Nov 1829
McKNIGHT, Asenath (Col. S.B.) of Cape Girardeau
            In Cape Girardeau 27 October by Horrell, J.P.

GREENWAY, George   20 August   JEFRE 23 Aug 1834
BROOKSHIRE, Mrs. Abigail   Benjamin M. Lisle

GRISWOLD, M. W.   2 April   MORE   6 Apr 1840
O'BANNON, Ann J. (only dau/John)   Rev. J. Rule

HACKLER, Samuel   5 August in Johnson Co.   MORE 17 Aug 1844
SMITH, Martha Ann (second dau/Harrison, of Lexington KY)
                      By Henry I. Pease, J.P.

HAINES, Josiah   10 December   LADB 14 Dec 1846
JOHNSON, Ann Elizabeth (Capt. T.T.)   Bacon, J.P.

HALE, George B. 21 March in Herculaneum   MORE   2 Apr 1840
SHEPPARD, Lucinda A.   Rev. William A. Walker
            "At the home of Mrs. Ellis." Both bride and
                   groom of Jefferson Co.

HALL, Charles W.   18 February in Marion Co.   PWH   2 May 1840
SMITH, Harriet (Thomas M.)   Merriel, J.P.

HALL, Robert P. of St. Louis   in Fredericksburg VA   NERA 14 Oct 1845
HALL, Charlotte (John B.) of Fredericksburg
                25 September by Rev. E. C. McGuire

HALL, Willard P.   28 October in St. Joseph   JEM 16 Nov 1847
RICHARDSON, Ann Eliza (Maj. William P.)
                No minister or J.P. shown.

HALLEY, Presley W. in Howard Co. 18 December   MIN 7 Dec 1827
PATRICK, Mrs. Ann   Rodgers, J.P.

HAMILL, Joseph   15 April   NERA 19 Apr 1845
JOHNSTON, Mary Jane (Samuel)   Rev. Dinwiddie
                "Pittsburgh please copy"

HAMILTON, J. Charles   24 March in Marion Co.   PWH 2 Apr 1842
HAYDEN, Martha (Dr. B. W.)   Rev. Dickson

HAMMOND, Allen, publisher of the Boonville Observer   MORE 24 Aug 1846
DUNCAN, Harriet Elizabeth (W.C.) of Jefferson City
        In Jefferson City, date or minister not shown.

HAMMOND, John   11 March   (widow of/)   NERA 15 Mar 1849
ROGERS, Mrs. Rebecca (Col. James, deceased) Rev. Buren

HANCOCK, Winfield S. of the U.S. Army 24 January   SLINT 28 Jan 1850
RUSSELL, Elmira (Eleanora?) (dau/Samuel, of St. Louis)
                By Rev. W. S. Eliot)

HANNA, William   in Nodaway Co., no date shown   JEM 20 Oct 1846
RICHARTS, Mrs. Mary   Caleb S. Burns, J.P.

HARDWICK, Johnson   in Marion Co. 5 January   PWH 9 Jan 1841
RHOADS, Catherine Ann (Daniel) Rev. Thomas P. Sharp

HARRINGTON, Frederick Thomas   15 April   MORE 20 Apr 1850
NEWELL, Charlotte (youngest dau/Joseph, of Nottingham Eng.)
                By Rev. James Lyon in Westminster Church.

HARRIS, Oliver, co-Editor of the Salt River Journal   PAMJ 21 May 1836
DUDLEY, Mary A.C. (John) late of Lincoln Co., formerly
                of Clark Co. KY)
        12 May at the home of Col. Parker Dudley,
                by Rev. Samuel Findley.

HARVEY, Thomas J.   9 January   BRUNS 13 Jan 1849
TOOLEY, Mary Jane (Charles P.) no minister or J.P. shown
                "all of Howard Co."

HARVEY, John   17 September   BRUNS 27 Sep 1849
MARKLAND, Eliza Ann (Levi) of Howard Co.
                No minister or J.P. shown.

HARWOOD, Levin B. of Russelville KY   "Tuesday"   SWERE 21 Sep 1846
MARMADUKE, Jane (Hon. M. M.)   in Saline Co.
                No minister or J. P. shown.

HATCHER, Thomas E.   23 November in Marion Co.   PWH 28 Nov 1840
HART, Martha Ann (Morgan)   Rev. E. Ballenger
                "Parents of the bride consenting."

HATCHITT, Rev. Leroy D. of the Christian Church   LADB 28 Dec 1846
ADAMS, Mary P. (Levin, deceased)   20 December
              By Rev. Greenup Jackman

HAWKINS, Alfred J.   18 September   HANJ 25 Sep 1851
HENNEGAR, Mrs. Rebecca   Rev. Benjamin Stevens
            "All of Marion Co."

HAWKINS, George W. of Hannibal in Ralls Co. 13 May   LADB 21 May 1851
PRIEST, Ann E. (Thomas) of Ralls Co. Rev. J. H. Lorance

HAWKINS, James G.   25 April in Palmyra   MORE 11 May 1830
COPPITT, Mary E. (Dr. E.)   Rev. Kitron

HAYDEN, L. F. of Lexington   Tuesday last   BRUNS 12 Aug 1848
DONOHUE, Susan M. (Stephen) of Howard Co.
           No minister or J.P. shown.

HEALY, D. B. of St. Louis   5 July   SLNL 10 Jul 1847
DONNELLY, Mary A. of Williamsborough MD   Fr. Kenney

HEISEN, Dr. F. A. A. of Bowling Green, Pike Co.   MORE 1 Nov 1837
PAXTON, Ann (eldest dau/Joseph, of Pike Co.)
        22 October by Rev. James Campbell.

HENDERSON, Alexander H. of Portland 15 March   MORE 27 Mar 1837
FINLEY, Hadassas (James, of Lincoln Co.) Rev. McAfee

HENDERSON, Capt. Andrew P.   12 September   JEM 28 Sep 1847
McKINNEY, Elizabeth J. (Rev. John)
        No minister or J. P. shown.

HENDERSON, George   10 November   MOAR 18 Nov 1836
HEATH, Jane Lee (youngest dau/Dr. William) Rev. Wallace
        "All of St. Louis Co."

HENDRICK, R. C. of Callaway Co. in St. Louis   BEA 18 Oct 1832
BOYD, Lucy Ann Rebecca (John) formerly of Lynchburg VA
       By Rev. A. McAllister, no date shown.

HENDRY, Charles F. of St. Louis   in Pittsburgh 14 May NERA 24 May 1845
KELLY, Annie F. (John)   Rev. O'Connor

HENRY, John W.   29 August   BRUNS 6 Sep 1849
WILLIAMS, Maria (Col.) no minister or J.P. shown
        "All of Fayette."

HERRIFORD, Andrew C. of St. Louis Co. 23 November SLDU 2 Dec 1847
STRICKLAND, Mary A. (Gen. E.B., of Franklin Co.)
      In Franklin Co., by Sam Bucker, J.P.

HICKMAN, W. L. of St. Louis Co. 5 January in St. Charles MORE 21 Jan 1848
WATSON, Ann Eliza (Dr. A.D., of St. Charles)
        By Rev. DeCoen

HIGGINS, Joseph C.   20 September   JEM 26 Sep 1848
DELLINGER, Ellen   Rev. Warren Wharton
      "At the home of Wm. C. Young."

HIGHTOWER, __ (not shown in paper, John R. in record) SPRIG 1 Sep 1849
McKOIN, Angeline (Thomas) 23 August, all of Springfield
      She is Sarah A. in record; no minister shown.

HILL, James A.   MODE 15-17 Nov 1847
WILCOX, Sarah (Dr. George B.) "all of Rocheport"
                    No date or minister shown.

HILL, Samuel Abel   10 June in Cape Girardeau Co.   JEM 22 Jun 1847
SLOAN, Julia Ann (Hiram) of Cape Girardeau Co.
                    By Rev. D. E. Y. Rice

HINKLE, Thomas   3 May   LEXA 9 May 1848
HOUSTON, Arabella (Abner and Sarah) Elder Henry Fisher
                    "All of this county."

HOARD, Dr. William Henry of Hannibal 2 December   FAME 13 Dec 1834
WILLIAMS, Ann W., late of Eastern Shore MD
                    By Rev. William Potts

HODGE, Josiah B. of Osage Co. 11 April   JEM 25 Apr 1848
SWOYER, Mrs. Maria of Cooper Co.   Rev. Douglas

HOFFMAN, Samuel   CGWE 17 Jan 1851
BURNS, Susan E.   Rev. D. F. Y. Rice
                    "At the home of I. R. Wathen."

HOKE, William   24 August in Marion Co.   PWH 2 Sep 1843
LEWIS, Frances (Jasper W.)
                    No minister or J.P. shown.

HOLDEN, Edward of St. Louis   16 September   NERA 18 Sep 1845
SINGLETON, Sarah Frances (Henry)   Rev. H. M. Field
                    Location of ceremony not shown.

HOLLINGSWORTH, Francis   30 June   HAG 8 Jul 1847
BOWER, Martha J. (3rd dau/Dr. G.M.)   Rev. Norman Parks
                    "All of Marion Co."

HOLT, Henry   24 January in Marion Co.   PWH 28 Jan 1843
OLDHAM, Mrs. Milly   Rev. Taylor

HOOVER, Dr. George W., formerly of Boone Co. MO   BRUNS 28 Oct 1848
WILLIAMS, Huldah E. (H., of Sullivan Co.)
                    10 October in Sullivan Co.

HOUSEMAN, James B.   23 December   SLDU 28 Dec 1846
WATSON, Emily (Thomas)   Rev. William Potts
                    "All of St. Louis."

HOUTS, C. B.   8 June, in the evening   CGWE 9 Jun 1848
EVANS, Mrs. E. J.   Rev. S. H. Ford

HOWARD, James   18 January   LEXP 28 Jan 1845
WILSON, Agnes, formerly of England Elder T.N. Gaines

HOWARD, Joseph B., a merchant of Columbia 24 May   MIN 31 May 1827
CUNNINGHAM, Sarah (James)   Rev. David Doyle

HOWELL, John of Calhoun Co. IL   16 September   LADB 24 Sep 1849
BUNN, Mrs. Sarah of Pike Co. MO   John Price, J.P.

HOWELL, William J. of Paris, MO. in Marion Co.   BRUNS 16 Sep 1848
GORE, Margaret A. (Jonathan, of Hannibal) in Hannibal
                    No minister or J. P. shown.

HUBBARD, E. H. of Batesville, Bates Co. AR   25 August   MORE   4 Sep 1847
SCOTT, Emily A. of Washington Co. MO   Rev. E. Colburn
            "At the home of John Scott in Cooper Co."

HUGHES, Charles J.   18 June in Kingston, Caldwell Co.   JEM 23 Jul 1850
POLLARD, Sarena (late Capt. W. C.)
                No minister or J.P. shown.

HUGHES, Tandy of Highland Co. OH   2 March   HAJ   9 Mar 1848
FUGATE, Nancy Ann of Ralls Co.   John M. Johnson, J.P.

HUGHES, William of Lancaster, MO. 16 August   MORE 30 Aug 1849
ROBINSON, Ann Elizabeth (Judge)   in Schuyler Co.
                No minister or J. P. shown.

HUMPHREYS, John (of Humphreys and Thatcher) 16 November   SLDU 19 Nov 1847
WALSH, Mary Ellen (Edward)   Fr. Holm

HUNT, George W. 1 September   COP   9 Sep 1842
HARRIS, Sarah (Overton)   Rev. R. S. Thomas

HUNTINGTON, George L., merchant of St. Louis   MOSN   7 Apr 1838
FORBES, Hannah F. of Boston
                No minister or J. P. shown.

HURT, Jubal   "Thursday last"   MIN 12 Jul 1827
CLARK, Patsey (Bennett)   Rev. Edward Turner

HUSTON (HUESTON), Robert, of Troy in Lincoln Co.   COMB 12 Oct 1835
TAYLOR, Caroline (Roger, of Warren Co.)
                October 7 by Rev. Thomas Bowen.

HUTCHESON, John   16 February in Howard Co.   BOLT 20 Feb 1841
RUCKER, Sarah Ann (William E.)   Elder H. L. Boon

HYDE, George A.   10 April   NERA 15 Apr 1845
EASBY, Cecelia J. (William, of Washington City)
                By Rev. Lutz

IMPEY, Elijah   1 October in Andrew Co.   JEM 20 Oct 1846
PARKER, Mrs. Joan   Rev. E. A. Carson

INGRAM, Thomas Sr. of St. Louis 19 May   BEA 27 May 1830
BERRIAN, Catherine W., formerly of NY   Rev. Lippincott
            "At the home of C. Wiggins in Illinois."

JACKSON, William C. of Shelby Co. 15 December in Monroe PWH 17 Dec 1842
SHARP, Emily E. (Richard) Rev. J. Lanius   /Co.
                "At Sharpsburg."

JAMESON, Horatio   18 November in Cole Co.   JEM 24 Nov 1846
HARTLY, Mrs. Frances   William M. Kerr, J. P.

JAMESON, James of Palmyra "Sunday last"   PAMC 21 Nov 1835
BUCKNER, Mrs. Susan F. of Monroe Co. Elder Henry Thomas

JAMESON, John of Fulton 23 February in Boone Co.   MOAR 10 Mar 1837
HARRIS, Susan (Major T.)   Rev. F. Wilhite

JEFFRIES, Elisha B.   10 April   JEM 30 Apr 1850
GREGORY, Mary N. (Roderick, at his home) Rev. Joseph Fenton
                    All of Franklin Co.

JENKINS, Aaron   4 February   MOAR 19 Feb 1836
FRISTOE, Mary Jane (Amos)   George Smith, J.P.
              Note: an Aaron Jenkins had previously married a Frances
                    Jenkins (Book A) and later an Ellen B. Miller
                    (Book B) prior to this, though it may not, of
                    course, have been the same man.

JENKINS, Col. Ephraim of Richmond VA   16 December   MORE 11 Jan 1831
McDOWEL, Margaret of Pike Co.
                    No minister or J.P. shown.

JENKINS, James A.   19 December "in the Big Bend"   CGWE 27 Dec 1850
WILKINSON, Serilda Ann (John S.) William Steinback, J.P.
                    All of Cape Girardeau Co.

JESSUP, J. B.   9 January in St. Louis   MORE 11 Jan 1850
JONES, Mrs. Madaline   Rev. Lewis

JOHNSON, A., merchant of Brunswick 15 June   BRUNS 24 Jun 1848
CABELL, Pocahontas (youngest dau/E. B.) in Keytesville
                    No minister or J. P. shown.

JOHNSON, Anderson   10 July   HWU 31 Jul 1851
BRIGGS, Mary Catherine (Rev. Samuel G.) Rev. Farnsworth
                    All of Scotland County.

JOHNSON, Edward   Tuesday last in Cape Girardeau   INP ca 1 Dec
YOUNG, Sally (Philip)   1826
                    No minister or J.P. shown.

JOHNSON, George A.   16 April   HAG 20 Apr 1848
THOMAS, Mrs. Malinda E.   Elder D. T. Morton

JOHNSON, James E.   "Thursday last"   COP 4 Dec 1841
PERSINGER, Sarah Ann (Alexander) Marcus Wills, J.P.

JOHNSON, John L.   date not shown   BOLT 25 May 1841
MARLEY, Nancy (Abel)   H. L. Boon
              "All of this place." (Fayette)

JOHNSON, R. S.   2 May at New Franklin   BOLT 16 May 1840
LEE, Catherine (Mrs. Sarah)   George C. Chapman, J.P.

JOHNSON, Capt Vincent P. 2 October in Cooper Co.   MIN 14 Oct 1823
ALLISON, Lucy (Ephraim)   Rev. Luke Williams

JOHNSON, William S.   in Marion Co., no date shown   PWH 3 Apr 1841
JOHNSON, Mrs. Ruth   William Maddox, J. P.

JOHNSON, Benjamin, age 70   31 August   FAME 11 Sep 1834
TYLER, Charlott of Big River Twp.   John Williams, J. P.
                    "Both of Jefferson Co."

JOHNSON, J. D.   10 December in St. Charles   JEFRE 20 Dec 1834
CHRISTY, Neville (Major William)
                    No minister or J. P. shown.

JONES, E. N.   8 October in Benton Co.   JEM 13 Oct 1846
STEWART, ___ (John)   Rev. Isaac W. K. Handy

JONES, G. C. of St. Louis at Jefferson City 1 September MORE 4 Sep 1849
BULLOCK, Mary C. (Col. Thealler of New Orleans)
                     No minister or J. P. shown.

JONES, George H.   8 May in Hannibal   LADB 21 May 1851
DRAPER, Maria (Judge Z. G.)   Rev. J. L. Bennett

JONES, Rev. Isaac, pastor of the Presbyterian Church   COP 12 Aug 1842
BOUCHELLE, Ellena M. (Dr. Thomas, decd, of Morgantown NC)
                 10 August by Rev. R. L. McAfee

JONES, James E.   17 December in Marion Co.   PWH 8 Jan 1845
NEAL, Martha Ann (James, decd)   Rev. John Young

KARNEY (KEARNEY), Andrew Jackson in Lewis Co.   MORE 16 Feb 1849
RANDOLPH, Susan A. (Col. Isaac, decd)   Rev. Moroin
               "16 January in LaGrange"

KAVANAUGH, Archibald   in Cooper Co. 11? 14? July   MIN 16 Jul 1821
EWING, Mary A. (Rev. Finis)   Rev. Robert Morrow

KELLY, William F.   1 May   MORE 4 May 1850
HAWKEN, Anna Maria (Samuel)   Rev. A. Bullard
            (Probably in St. Louis or St. Louis Co.)

KELSO, Edward B. of Scott Co.   "Thursday last"   JASO 15 Sep 1838
BYRD, Nancy (Capt. Abraham, of Cape Girardeau Co.)
          In Cape Girardeau Co. by Rev. Peter Williams.

KENNEDY, Alexander S. of St. Louis in New York City   NERA 4 Apr 1849
BENNETT, Elizabeth Ann   Rev. Sillick
            14 March at Mariners Methodist Church.

KERNS, Dr. A.   22 August   SJA 30 Aug 1850
BOYER, Alcinda (Peter)   Rev. S. H. Kerns
                 All of Buchanan Co.

KERR, Dr. James A.   5 June   MIN 14 Jun 1827
BELL, Martha (Col. John M.)   Rev. Samuel Davis

KERR, William D.   13 October in Jefferson City   NERA 24 Nov 1845
CALLAHAN, Mrs. Henrietta S.
                 No minister or J. P. shown.

KIDD, William R.   15 February   HAJ 22 Feb 1849
PITTS, Sarah Elizabeth (James P.)   Rev. Benjamin Stephens
                 All of Hannibal.

KINCAID, Andrew H. 18 February in Marion Co.   PWH 19 Feb 1845
BARNETT, Rachel (Enoch D.) Rev. Samuel B. F. Caldwell

KINCAID, James   20 December   LADB 31 Dec 1849
MARTIN, Martha Ann (eldest dau/James M.) Rev. J. W. Campbell
                 All of Pike Co.

KING, Hon. A. of St. Charles   "Wednesday last"   JEM 15 Jun 1847
BASYE, Narcissa (Alfred, of Jefferson City)
                 By Rev. Bullard

KING, Barnabas B.   15 May in Marion Co.   PWH 18 May 1844
CARNEGY, Matilda Louise (S. W. B.) Rev. Samuel D. Rice

KING, George of St. Louis   in Manchester MO 19 Oct. NERA 25 Nov 1845
THOMAS, Elizabeth (Phineas)   Rev. John B. Browne
              "She of Franklin Co., formerly of
                          Hardy Co. VA."

KING, John   23 September   SLDU 25 Sep 1847
RAYNOR, Cordelia (step-d/George Barrow) Rev. Caples

KINGSBURY, Horace (Noah?)   BRUNS 21 Oct 1847
ALLEN, Mrs. Icybindy   no minister or J.P. shown
              (The newspaper might have erred here, as he is shown
                  as Horace in the record and Noah in the newspaper.)

KNOX, Dr. William J. 1 April in Lincoln Co.   MORE 7 Apr 1846
BROWNING, Sarah L. (William W.) Elder Thomas Wright

KRING, John N.   "Tuesday last"   MODE 9/7 Dec 1846
CRIGLAR, Sarah Ann (Lewis) Rev. William G. Caples

KUMBERT, John J.   18 November   MOSN 1 Dec 1838
VOGT, Mrs. Augusta   Justice McKenney
                    "Both of this city."

LA BEAUME, Peter of Ralls Co. in Shelbyville 27 March PWH 2 Apr 1842
VANDIVER, Joyce B. (Samuel) formerly of VA
                  No minister or J. P. shown.

** LADEW, Charles "one of the proprietors of the Peoples'
                  Organ" 19 August in St. Louis   JEM 24 Aug 1847
CONDON, Elizabeth (Richard, decd) Rev. Van Court

LAKE, Jeptha   25 March in Marion Co.   PWH 3 Apr 1841
BROWN, Susan (Anderson) no minister or J. P. shown

LAMME, David S.   in Boone Co. "last Tuesday"   MIN 27 Mar 1829
HICKMAN, Mrs. Sophia   Rev. W. Cochran

LANDIS, Israel   3 May   MOAR 6 May 1836
STIBBS, Sarah (3rd dau/Christopher) Rev. Geo. W. Bewley

LANSDOWN, Dr. George W. 24 February   JEFRE 7 Mar 1835
DIXON, M. A. (Warren)   Hon. George Tompkins

** LAREW, Charles of "People's Organ" date illegible   HAG 2 Sep 1847
GORDON, Elizabeth (R., decd)   Rev. Van Court

        A puzzler. The published marriage records of St. Louis do
    not show this marriage; they show a Charles Laderr marrying
    an Elizabeth Condon in 1846, and an Elizabeth Condon wed to
    Charles Luden in 1847(?). However, an Elizabeth Ladew, wife
    of Charles died in 1857 ae 28, and this is possibly the
    couple shown. Best guess: Charles Ladew, Elizabeth Condon.

LAWLESS, Byrd   in Howard Co., no date shown   MIN 18 Dec 1824
SCOTT, Eliza G. "at the residence of Samuel Hughes."
                  by Ebenezer Rodgers

LAWRENCE, George P. in Marion Co. 11 December   PWH 18 Dec 1845
MORTON, Mehitable (Samuel)   Broaddus (JP? Rev.?)

LAWLER, William   16 May   MOSN 19 May 1838
BOLAND, Mrs. Catherine   Justice McKenney

LEE, Woodruff, of Palmyra, at Jacksonville IL   LADB 24 Feb 1851
AILSMAN, Sarah (Andrew) of Jacksonville
                    No date or minister shown.

LEEPER, James   15 March   BRUNS 31 Mar 1849
GRAVES, Elizabeth (John) "all of Chillicothe"
                    No minister or J. P. shown.

LEEPER, Samuel G.   27 January   BRUNS 3 Feb 1848
JEFFREYS, Ellen Frances (Coleman) no minister shown
                    "All of Brunswick Twp."

LEEPER, William E.   14 February   BRUNS 17 Feb 1849
ASHBY, Eliza J. (James S.) no minister or J.P. shown

LEET, Daniel, formerly of Washington PA   5 June   J-MOH 7 Jun 1845
KELSAY, Juliet, formerly of Troy NY   Rev. Lewis
          At the home of John Heard by Rev. Lewis.

LEGG (LEGGS), Mathew 31 January in St. Louis   MORE 2 Feb 1850
GUELBERTH (GILBERT), Zelina (eldest dau/August)
                    By Fr. Paris.

LEMMON, Andrew, formerly of Harford Co. MD   MORE 21 Sep 1849
BRISCOE, Mary Jane   19 September by Rev. Pollock

LEWIS, James of St. Louis   9 May   SLDU 12 May 1847
HOLLMAN, Emily of Salem MA   Elder J. M. Grant

LEWIS, James P.   in Cooper Co. 18 November   COMB 26 Nov 1847
MANN, Phebe (Jacob)   Rev. T. A. Ish
                    "All of this county."

LEWIS, Joseph F.   14 March   PWH 18 Mar 1843
McCORMICK, Amanda Adeline (Samuel)   A. Broaddus

LEWIS, Samuel   18 May   MOAR 27 May 1836
WASH, Mildred D. (3rd dau/Thomas) Rev. Smulling?

LEWIS, Thomas A. of Old Jefferson, MO   19 April   MOSN 21 Apr 1838
BURD, Martha J. O. (William) of St. Louis Rev. Ames

LIGGETT, Stephen of Howard Co. 2 August   MODE 22/20 Sep 1847
SAPPINGTON, Anna (James) of Saline Co.
                    No minister or J. P. shown.

LINDLEY, Malcolm A.   9 October   HAJ 11 Oct 1849
COCHRAN, Sophia P. (Rev. William P.) Rev. Lorance
          "Burlington, Quincy, and St. Louis please copy."

LINDSAY, James, of Cape Girardeau, in Madison Co.   MORE 1 Nov 1838
FRYER, Caroline (Robert M.) of Madison Co.
                    4 October by Rev. Polk.

LITTLE, James A. of St. Louis in Morristown NJ   NERA 16 Aug 1845
MARTIN, Catherine G. of Morristown
          15 July by Rev. Thomas McCarrol

McAFEE (MACKFEE), Edward   16 December near Hermann   SLINQ 31 Dec 1849
WILSON, Mrs. Zarilda (James Gunsollis)   Rev. Kippes
            (Published record shows her as Zelda.)

McCABE, Dr. J. Kellie (Keder) of Georgetown, Pettis Co. COMB 26 Nov 1847
McBRIDE, Eliza Jane (Judge) of Paris MO.
            18 November by Rev. S. C. McConnell in
                                    Monroe Co.
    Note: the marriage above also appears in HAG, 26 Nov. This
          shows the groom as Dr. Joseph and the bride as the
          daughter of the Hon. P. H. McBride.

McCOMAC, James, formerly of Ireland 5 September   MOAR 10 Sep 1839
HARRIS, Eliza, formerly of KY   no minister shown
          "At the home of Mr. Stamps of St. Louis in the
            presence of relatives, friends, and acquaintances."

McCORD, James, merchant of Clarksville 5 September   MORE 17 Sep 1833
PEPPER, Edna (Samuel) in Pike Co. by Rev. Hughes

McCORMICK, William J.   no date shown   SLOB 31 Mar 1836
TERRELL, Margaret M. at the home of James Terrell
            Both of Marion Co.; by Rev. S. C. McConnell

McCOY, Joseph   20 February in Marion Co.   PWH 5 Mar 1842
THORP (THARP?), Susan at the home of G. McDaniel
            By Rev. T. E. Paine

McCUNE, John (William)   5 February   LADB 11 Feb 1850
TAPLEY, Louisa (Green)   Rev. A. Allison
            All of Pike Co.

McDANNOLD, Newton   14 October   LADB 18 Oct 1847
McCUNE, Mrs. Martha C.   Elder A. D. Landram
            All of Pike Co.

McDONALD, Allen B.   9 October in Marion Co.   PWH 15 Oct 1842
DARR, Mrs. Emily   A. Broaddus

McDONALD, Isaac W. (or P.)   "Thursday"   BRUNS 20 Jan 1849
MALLORY, Analetta P. (W. T.) at Fayette Christian Church

McDONNEL, Edward C.   10 March in Hannibal   PWH 12 Mar 1842
PEAKE, Susan (Humphrey)   Rev. T. E. Paine

McDOWELL, John   in Howard Co., no date   MIN 23 Jul 1822
WEILS (WELLS), Mrs. Jemima (Col. F. Trammell)
                    By Augustus Storrs

McGINNIS, Smith, of Lincoln Co.   15 February   LADB 21 Feb 1848
CLARK, Mrs. V. G., of Pike Co. Rev. James W. Campbell

McKELLOPS, Dr. H. J. B.   3 April   NERA 6 Apr 1849
GOWER, Anna (R. L.)   Rev. Potts

McKENNY, J. H., a printer   20 November   FAME 27 Nov 1834
DUVALL, Mary P. (S. V.)   Rev. E. F. Hatfield

McKENZIE, Roderick Charles   15 August   SJA 16 Aug 1850
McKEE, Mrs. Bridget Martha Roy Rev. Thomas Scanlan

McPHEETERS, Dr. William M.   10 May   NERA 11 May 1849
BUCHANAN, Sallie (George)   Rev. E. C. Hutchinson

McPIKE, Abraham   17 December   LADB 21 Dec 1846
MORRIS, Margaret H.   Elder W. McQuie
          "At the home of Simeon B. Robinson in Bowling Green."

McQUITTY, Andrew Jackson   21 March   COGL 24 Mar 1848
HAWKINS, Elizabeth (James) no minister or J. P. shown

McWILLIAMS, James G.   24 July   HWU 31 Jul 1851
BUSH, Elizabeth I. (eldest dau/John)   D. T. Morton
                 All of Marion Co.

MABEN, William P. "Wednesday evening last"   JEFRE 27 Aug 1842
BOLTON, Mary Ann (Meriwether L.)   Rev. Noland

MADDOX, John W.   18 January   BOLT 22 Jan 1842
RAWLINS, Mary Ann (eldest dau/Judge Owen)
          All of Howard Co.; by Rev. Thomas Fristoe.

MAHAN, George G.   26 September in Palmyra   MORE 2 Oct 1848
HOYT, Sarah P. (David)   Rev. Leighton

MAHAN, M. J. of Cooper Co.   JEFRE 16 Mar 1844
RUMSEY, Mrs. M. of Cole Co.   Rev. M. D. Noland

MAJOR, James N. of Fayette   "Thursday last"   WEM 26 Mar 1840
BERNARD, Frances (I. N., of Cooper Co.)
                 By Rev. Hampton Boon

MAJOR, Samuel C. "Thursday last" in Howard Co.   MIN 6 Mar 1829
DALY, Elizabeth (Lawrence J.)   Ebenezer Rodgers

MARTIN, Maj. Alexander H.   8 December   LADB 23 Dec 1850
WRIGHT, Catherine A. (Elder Thomas J.) Rev. D. T. Sherman
                 All of Lincoln Co.

MARTIN, Faulkland H. 15 April in Jefferson City   MORE 18 Apr 1846
DUNKLIN, Emilie S. (Gov. Daniel)   Rev. Cowan

MARTIN, James B.   24 July   SLDU 1 Aug 1848
ECKLER, Mrs. F. S.   Rev. Parks
                 Both of St. Louis.

MARTIN, Dr. James M. of Florissant   BEA 31 Mar 1831
WALTON, Nancy (George)   Joel Musick
                 All of St. Louis Co.

MARTIN, John T., formerly of Baltimore 22 May   MOSN 26 May 1838
SPENCE, Precilla (Henry) of St. Louis   Rev. Ames

MARTIN, Joseph   "Tuesday evening last"   MIN 16 Oct 1821
CARSON, Mrs. Rebecca   Augustus Storrs
                 In Howard Co.

MARTIN, Murdock   Sunday in Howard Co.   BOLT 31 Oct 1840
TITUS, Arethusa (Ebenezer) Rev. Thomas Campbell
          (Rev. Campbell shown as "of Cole Co.")

MASSEY, John B. of Canton in Hannibal 25 November   HAG 26 Nov 1846
DAVIS, Mary C. E. (Mrs. Martha) Rev. W. N. Crawford

MASSEY, Capt. Nathan of Indian Creek Twp., 6 January   LADB 17 Jan 1848
DUNCAN, Mrs. Susan A.   A. J. Davis, J. P.
            All of Pike Co.

MASSEY, William   18 February in Ralls Co.   HAG 25 Feb 1847
FORD, Mrs. Matilda   Rev. Light
          At the home of William Maddox.

MASSIE, Henry A., merchant of St. Louis   22 June   MORE 7 Jul 1829
MASSIE, Nancy D. (Samuel)   no minister or J.P. shown
         At Merrimack Iron Works, in Crawford Co.

MAUZE, Jacob P.   8 December   JEFRE 18 Dec 1841
BUCHHOLTZ, Mrs. Catherine   no minister or J. P. shown
         Both of Jefferson City.

MAXFIELD, Andrew H.   17 February   MORE 22 Feb 1842
SULLIVAN, Mildred (Joseph, of Lincoln Co.)
         By Elder Thomas Wright

MELLON, Jessemon   30 November   COP 4 Dec 1841
SUTTON, America (Ben)   Rev. George M. Effinger
         All of Boone Co.

MEREDITH, Absalom   2 November   BORE 21 Nov 1843
MOSS, Nancy M. (Capt E.)   Rev. Wallice
         All of Cooper Co.

MEREDITH, Charles L.   23 April   JEFRE 25 Apr 1835
GORDEN, Sarah (Alexander)   Hiram H. Baber

MICHAU, Alfred, of St. Louis   13 March   SJA 14 Mar 1851
SAUNDERS, Nannie J. (John, of Maryville)
         By Rev. T. S. Reeve, in St. Joseph.

MILLER, George W.   12 July   LADB 16 Jul 1849
NEARNS, Mrs. Mary   John C. Massie, Esq.
         All of Louisiana, MO.

MILLER, Henry B., formerly of Rappahannock Co. VA   COMB 9 Dec 1847
BROWN, Pamelia (Thomas G.)   Rev. A. Pattison
         On 2 December; all of Howard Co.

MILLER, Robert H., editor of the Tribune 28 June   BRUNS 8 Jul 1848
PETERS, Enfield F. (John R.) in Clay Co.
         No minister shown; Miller was probably the
         editor of the Liberty Tribune.

MILLER, Thomas P.   22 December   JEFRE 25 Dec 1841
WINSTON, Louisa (Nicholas)   no minister or J.P. shown

MILLER, William   in Cooper Co., no date shown   MIN 28 Jan 1823
MITCHELL, Agnes (Capt. Thomas)   Rev. R. Morrow

MINOR, J. L., Secretary of State   27 February   MORE 4 Apr 1844
GOOD, Sarah (Thomas, deceased)   Rev. Chandler
         /of Cole Co.

MINOR, Col. N. P. of Pike Co.   in Christian Co. KY   LADB 25 Dec 1848
LEWIS, Susan M., recently of Albemarle Co. VA
         At the home of John H. Morris, on 2 December,
            by Rev. Tucker.

MITCHELL, John, of St. Louis   13 May in St. Louis   MOAR 20 May 1840
BROOKS, Louisa of Philadelphia   Rev. Smith

MOFFETT, E. M. of Hannibal   14 January   HAG 21 Jan 1847
COX, Sarah M. (Jonathan) of Monroe Co.   Dr. McConnell

MOONYHAM, C. Erwin   12 March in Lafayette Co.   MORE 23 Mar 1837
HERD, Jane (2nd dau/John)   William Allison, Esq.

MOORE, Dr. Alexander "Tuesday last" in Farmington   MORE 29 Sep 1836
BOYCE, Jane (John)   Rev. Van Doren
                All of Farmington, St. Francois Co.

MOORE, Nelson   no date   FAME 21 Feb 1835
CROW, Elouise (Hugh) late of VA   Rev. Herley

MOORE, Thomas   21 May   MOSN 26 May 1838
BRAIL, Mrs. Christina   Justice McKenney

MORELAND, H. E.   14 December   SLDU 18 Dec 1848
NELSON, Mrs. Mary L.   Rev. Linn
                "Both of this city."

MORIN, John   25 November in Howard Co.   COMB 16 Dec 1847
CRIGLAR, Jemima (Richard)   John Harvey, Esq.

MORRIS, David   4 November   COMB 19 Nov 1847
TAYLOR, Mary S. (Thornton) no minister or J.P. shown

MORRIS, John P.   21 November in Howard Co.   MIN 25 Nov 1823
HUGHES, Mary I. (eldest dau/William) Ebenezer Rodgers
                All of Howard Co.

MORRISON, Alfred M. 15 March in Howard Co.   MIN 20 Mar 1825
JACKSON, Minerva (Capt. John) Ebenezer Rodgers

MORTON, John, of St. Louis   8 October   MORE 14 Oct 1849
WILBURNE, Mrs. Mary, of Nashville Rev. A. Bullard
            (Probably in St. Louis, where Bullard was
                a minister for a number of years.)

MOSELY, James   10 October   LADB 14 Oct 1850
HENDRICKS, Nancy (Johnson)   Rev. William F. Watson
            Both of Bowling Green, Pike Co.

MOSS, Lieut. James H. of Liberty   in Columbia   MORE 18 Oct 1847
WOODSON, Susan A. (Judge Warren)   on 30 September
                By Elder T. M. Allen

MUGGAH, Charles H. 23 July in Cooper Co.   COMB 30 Jul 1846
FERRIOT, Mrs. Sarah H.   Rev. Griffin
                "Both of Attackapus, LA."

MUMFORD, Lieut. F. S.   at Jefferson Barracks   SLDU 1 Oct 1847
CALLAHAN, Jane B. (adopted dau/Col. Staniford)
            28 September by Rev. Corbin

MURRAY, E. C., Editor of the Banner   CANE 6 Dec 1849
LUCE, Marian B. (eldest dau/William) Rev. Lewy Hatchett
            In Louisiana, MO

MURRAY, George B. 3 March in St. Louis   MORE 6 Mar 1850
WATTS, Mrs. Sarah M.   Bishop Kenrick

MURRAY, S. F. of Bowling Green   29 January in Troy   JEM   8 Feb 1848
WELLS, Fanny (Carty) of Palmyra
                    No minister or J. P. shown.

NAPTON, William B., Attorney General   27 March   JEFRE 31 Mar 1838
WILLIAMS, Malinda (Judge) of Knoxville TN
              In Saline Co., by Rev. Boon.

NAYLOR, John F.   1 May   NERA 23 May 1849
SCOTT, Vesta (Lyman)   Rev. Post

NEAL, Thomas   14 March   CGWE 15 Mar 1850
BENNET, Mary   Rev. John H. Clark
              At the home of John Brooks.

NEELY, J. H. of Neely's Landing   5 June   CGWE 5 Jun 1849
HOPE, Margaret M.   no minister or J. P. shown
          At the home of Thomas Harris on Apple Creek.

NELSON, Dr. D. P. of St. Louis   18 August   BEA 1 Sep 1851
DUDGEON, Margaret of Cincinnati   P. Walsh, Esq.

NELSON, Col. Thomas   29 November   JEM 15 Dec 1846
ALEXANDER, Mrs. Eliza Jane   Elder H. Thomas

NENNSTIEL, Edward   17 September   MORE 20 Sep 1851
ROBERTSON, Mrs. Sophia   Bishop Hawks

NESBIT, Thomas, of Fulton   in Boone Co. 2 December   JEM 21 Dec 1847
BRYAN, Mrs. Mary   no minister or J. P. shown

NETHERLAND, Col. Richard, of Shelby Co. 17 March   PWH 19 Mar 1842
READ, Mrs. Mary Jane   Rev. J. Taylor
              At the home of Mrs. Sarah Phillips.

NETHERTON, Col. G. H.   22 March   MORE 24 Mar 1843
HARRISON, Ann Eliza (Jason)   Rev. Noland
                    In Jefferson City.

NEWMAN, John   5 July   BEA 12 Jul 1832
DUBREVILLE, Olympe (Antoine)   Rev. Lutz

NICHOLSON, Joseph   "Wednesday last"   PAMJ 28 May 1836
ALLEN, Zerelda (Thomas)   James J. Jamieson, Esq.
                    All of Palmyra.

NISBET, Robert N. of St. Louis   in Petersburg VA   NERA 25 Apr 1849
LEMOINE, Mary Good. 12 April, Rev. Benjamin H. Rice

NORRIS, William H. 12 April in Pleasant Hill*   BOLT 16 Apr 1842
SPENNY, Mary W. (Weedon)   Rev. Thatcher
              "All formerly of Fauquier Co. VA."
                 * in Cooper Co.

NORTH, William   19 February   FAME 28 Feb 1835
WILLIAMSON, Nancy M. (Charles, deceased) Rev. Bewley
              At the house of Lewis Nunn; "all of
                    Franklin County."

OLIVER, Alexander   10 May in Dayton OH   SLOB 2 Jun 1836
WUNDERLICH, Susan (Col. Jacob) of Dayton Rev. Gray

ONAN, Dennis   16 May   in Marion Co.   PWH 18 May 1844
MADDOX, Elizabeth (Bazil)   Rev. John Orange

O'NEIL, John, of Chester IL in Lebanon IL 2 April   SLDU 15 Apr 1848
ENGLISH, Mary Catherine (E.) of St. Louis
                By Rev. Griswold

O'SULLIVAN, Jeremiah   12 December?   SLDU 24 Dec 1846
O'SULLIVAN, Mrs. Ellen   Justice Black
                Both of St. Louis Co.

OWENS, Henry   8 June in Pike Co.   NERA 17 Jun 1845
BARNETT, Mrs. Mary   no minister or J. P. shown

OWENS, Joseph, of St. Louis   15 February   CGWE 16 Dec 1849
BROOKS, Amanda (John) of Cape Girardeau Co.
          By Rev. William F. Nelson, at the home of the
                bride's father.

PAGE, Joseph   20 May in Howard Co.   BOLT 22 May 1841
CRIGLER, Elizabeth (Lewis)   Elder W. Duncan
                All of Fayette.

PAINE, John W.   5 August in Lawrence Co.   JEM 17 Aug 1847
MATTHEWS, Ann (William)   Rev. Abel Burton

PAPIN, Timothy L.   23 January   MORE 24 Jan 1850
GARLAND, Mary L. (eldest dau/Hugh A.) Rev. Eliot

PARKER, Peter, of Hannibal, in Ralls Co. 17 October   HAJ 25 Oct 1849
BOYCE, Mary E. (3d dau/Judge Richard) Rev. J. Lanius
                "Romney VA please copy."

PARKS, Samuel L. B.   20 February in Howard Co.   BRUNS 3 Mar 1849
WINN, Dicey (William) no minister or J. P. shown

PARKS, Dr. Thomas   in Boonville 20 April   MIN 4 May 1830
HARTT, Sarah (Dr. George C.) Rev. Kavanaugh

PARRISH, Dr, H. M. of Springfield Tuesday last   SPRIG 21 Jul 1849
COLLINS, Mrs. Sarah J., of Butler Co. KY
                By Rev. B. McCord Reeves

PARRISH, Dr. Jeptha C.   19 August?   MODE 19 Aug 1847
TURNER, Elizabeth (James Sr.) Rev. Archibald Patison

PARROTT, Joseph V.   in Weston 4 November   JEM 1 Dec 1846
RAILEY, Pocahontas (Col. D. M.)   Rev. Steele
          Note: SLDU says Col. Daniel M. Railey, late
                of Abingdon VA.

PATTERSON, James H., formerly of Washington City   PWH 26 Mar 1842
ELY, Mary Ann Miles (youngest dau/Dr. Ezra Stiles Ely)
          By Dr. Ely, at West Ely, 20 March.

PAXTON, John A.   19 May   BGRAD 27 May 1843
WHITE, Dorcas   Rev. J. F. Gray
          In Montgomery Co., whose records burned.

PEASE, Joseph, a merchant   "Thursday"   SLOB 13 Nov 1834
CHENIE, Athalie (Antoine)   Rev. Lutz

PEAY, William   16 November   LADB 30 Nov 1846
LUCK, Mildred (Diggs)   Rev. Thomas T. Jackson

PECK, John W.   8 October   SLDU 10 Oct 1846
BOSWELL, Ann Shuter (2nd dau/Charles) Rev. A. Bullard

PEGRAM, E. T. W. 11 November in Howard Co.   JEM 1 Dec 1846
CRANE, Mildred Ann (George W., of Montgomery Co.)
                    By Rev. D. T. Sherman

PENNY, Dr. Eli of Caldwell Co. 12 February   LEXP 4 Mar 1845
HILL, Mary (Rev. Hill of Clay Co.) Rev. Philip Burris

PERKINS, Maj. Elihu H.   15 November   MORE 26 Nov 1838
RIGGS, Avice (2nd dau/Jonathan, of Lincoln Co.)
                    By Rev. Wadsworth

PERKINS, Walter (or Walton?) 25 May in Lincoln Co.   MORE 16 Jun 1834
GRIMES?, Louisiana (Robert)   Rev. Ball

PERRY, William S.   in Marion Co. 19 December   PWH 25 Dec 1845
McDANIEL, Martha Jane (Maj. William) Rev. W. D. Pollock

PEYTON, F. S., late of VA   15 December   BOBS 17 Dec 1840
ROSS, Mrs. Lucretia C.   Rev. Ball
                In the Presbyterian Church.

PHILLIPPEE, David   30 March   COP 9 Apr 1842.
MAYO, Mrs. Jane   Rev. George M. Effinger

PHILLIPS, William   in Cooper Co. 30 March   COMB 1 Apr 1847
SAMUEL, Mrs. Virginia   J. M. Edgar, Esq.

PIERCE, Charles S., formerly of Rappahannock Co. VA MODE 12/10 Aug 1846
BROYLES, Martha C., formerly of Madison Co. VA
                Wednesday last, near Fayette, by
                    Rev. Thomas Johnson.

PIERCE, John M., of Howard Co.   13 April   LADB 8 May 1848
JOHNSON, Nancy (Benjamin, of Pike Co.) Rev. Hardy

PIKE, Edward C., of St. Louis   25 October   MORE 26 Oct 1849
WILLIAMS, Harriet A., of Hyde Park, NY
            By Rev. E. C. Hutchinson, St. George's Church.

PILE, J. R., publisher of the Lexington Appeal   JEM 13 Oct 1846
HULETT, Mrs. Mary J. in Saline Co. 14 September
                No minister or J. P. shown.

PITTMAN, David K., of St. Charles in St. Louis   SLOB 25 Dec 1834
BAKER, Eliza, of St. Louis, late of Winchester VA
            By Rev. Edwin F. Hatfield, no date shown.

PLATT, John M., of St. Louis   2 May   MORE 6 May 1844
STOUT, Laura E. (Ira, of Walnut Grove, near Hannibal)
                By Rev. Samuel Rice

POINDEXTER, Theodore, formerly of Pittsburg IL   MORE 13 Jun 1850
WETHERILL, Ann L.   11 June, Rev. J. B. Townsend

POINTER, John L., formerly of Lynchburg VA   MOSN 5 Jan 1839
SLAUGHTER, Caroline E. of Plaquemine, Iberville Parish
            10 December by Judge Taylor   /LA

PORTER, Joseph, of Lewis Co. in Marion Co. 4 April   PWH 13 Apr 1844
MARSHALL, Mary Ann (Willis)   Elder Ballinger

POTEET, Samuel G. of Clay Co.   MORE 26 Feb 1833
BURCKHARTT, Elizabeth (Joshua H.) late of St. Louis Co.
          10 January by Robert B. Harrison, Esq.

POWELL, Albert   31 December in Warren Co.   MORE 9 Jan 1847
EDWARDS, Sarah O. M.   Rev. Black
          At the home of Maj. Brice Edwards.

POWELL, Barton Francis, of Hannibal 26 December   HAJ 4 Jan 1849
WILLINGHAM, Lucinda (John) of Mexico MO
          By Rev. Robert C. Mansfield

POWELL, Thomas W.   in Saline Co., no date shown   MODE 12 Jan 1848
SMITH, Louisa (Maj. William) no minister or J.P. shown

PRATHER, Philip age 68   7 April   MODE 14/12 Apr 1847
WALKUP, Margaret age 14 no minister or J.P. shown

PRATTE, Francis (Joseph and Mary) of Perry Co.   MORE 11 Dec 1838
COX, Cora (2nd dau/Caleb and Louisa) 6 November
          By Rev. Cline, in Fredericktown.

PREWITT, Dr. Robert C.   3 April   LADB 6 May 1850
SHAW, Lucy E. (William, deceased) Rev. William Barnett

PRIESTLY, Samuel   7 November in Jackson Co.   JEM 23 Nov 1847
WILCOX, Mrs. Mary no minister or J. P. shown

PYATT, Benjamin 29 March in Marion Co.   PWH 2 Apr 1842
LEWIS, Mrs. Mary   Elder L. Hatchett

QUARLES, Benjamin L.   3 May   HAJ 17 May 1849
YOUNG, Sarah E. (eldest dau/Rev. John F.)
          "All of Florida, Monroe Co." Rev. B. H. Spencer

RAINS, Allen   13 May in Howard Co.   BOLT 22 May 1841
DOUGLASS, Margaret (William)   Rev. Boon
          All of Howard Co.

RAMSEY, Allen   "Sunday evening last"   JEM 4 May 1846
KERR, Agnes E. (William M.)   Rev. J. H. Linn
          All of Cole Co.

RANSOM, Walter   2 April   NERA 4 Apr 1845
HUMPHREYS, Sarah Ann (James)   Rev. Griswold

RAY, Joseph C.   3 March   BOLT 19 Mar 1842
JOHNSON, Mary A. J., formerly of Lynchburg VA
          At the home of W. N. Feazel, Monticello, by
                  Dr. Calhoun.

RAY, William H., of New York, Schuyler Co. IL   MOSN 9 Jun 1838
CONINGHAM, Jane H. of Schuyler Co. IL
          Wednesday, by Rev. James Young.

RECTOR, Thomas   17 April at Jefferson Barracks   SLDU 29 Apr 1848
RIGGINS, Mrs. Frances (Maj. P. Morrison, USA)
          By Fr. Bourlandi?

REED, Preston B.   17 March   COP 27 Mar 1841
TATE, Mary F. (Maj. James)   Rev. John L. Yantis
          At the home of Maj. Daniel Nolly in Fulton.
              (Item from the Fulton Reformer)

REED, Silas, formerly of Cincinnati   15 May   MOSN 19 May 1838
RODGERS, Henrietta M. of Gloucester MA Rev. A. Bullard

REED, Warren A.   29 June in Marion Co.   PWH 2 Jul 1842
McCORMIC, Candace (eldest dau/Gordon) Rev. H.P. Goodrich

REILLY, Michael   19 April   NERA 22 Apr 1845
McGOWAN, Sarah, formerly of Philadelphia Rev. Allen

REILY, Dr. Philip B.   1 May   MORE 3 May 1850
FOSTER, Octavia (Joseph)   Bishop Kenrick

RENICK, Dr. O. F. of Carroll Co. 8 November   JEM 23 Nov 1847
RENICK, Sarah (Rev. Robert)   in Lexington
              Published records show his name as Oscar F.,
              the ceremony performed by William Lankford.

REYNOLDS, Ambrose D. of Fayette "Wednesday evening"   JEFRE 18 May 1844
BASYE, Frances W. (Maj. Alfred) of Jefferson City
              By Rev. W. T. Chandler

REYNOLDS, Dr. Loring Henry of KY 20 November   MORE 26 Nov 1844
CLEVELAND, Juliet Maria (Judah, or Capt. J. T.)
              At Hazel Ridge Cottage, Howard Co., by
                  Rev. Thomas Fristoe.

RHODES, Samuel H. of Rappahannock Co. VA   26 May   PWH 4 Jun 1842
THURMAN, Susan M. (Jeptha)   Rev. S. C. McConnell
              In Warren Twp., Marion Co.

RICE, W.   8 August   JEM 17 Aug 1847
THOMAS, Susan (George H.)   Elder Jacob Coons

RICHARDSON, J. C.   16 February in Cooper Co.   COMB 18 Feb 1847
LIONBERGER, Mary Elizabeth (Isaac) Rev. T. C. Harris
                  All of Boonville.

RICHARDSON, William B.   3 December   NERA 7 Jan 1846
McDONALD, Mrs. Maria   Rev. Galbreath
                  All of St. Louis Co.

RIDDLE, Col. A.   3 April   NERA 5 Apr 1845
TREADWAY, Mary (Capt. Harvey of Middletown CT)
                  By Rev. A. Bullard

RIGBY, David, of Vicksburg "Tuesday morning last"   CGWE 6 Dec 1850
GORDON, Mrs. Eliza M. (Mrs. Lucy Henderson)
              No minister or J. P. shown.

RIGGINS, William P.   21 December   JEFRE 25 Dec 1841
SOAN, Sarah (Michael) no minister or J. P. shown

RITCHEY, Lemuel J., of the Warsaw Visitor   JEM 1 Dec 1846
DEFORD, Martha A. (Rev. Joseph M.) in Benton Co.
              22 November; no minister or J. P. shown.

ROBBINS, Z. C., a merchant   12 January   MOAR 13 Jan 1837
TILDEN, Mary Jane (R. S.) late of Lynchburg VA
                   By Rev. Tabor

ROBBISON, Hardy   11 August in Jefferson City   JEFRE 17 Aug 1833
RIGGINS, Minerva (James)   H. H. Baber

ROBERTS, Dr. John W.   2 September   COP 4 Sep 1841
KIRBY, Jenetta S. (Jehu) Rev. George M. Effinger

ROBINSON, John W. of Callaway Co.   26 March   LEXP 22 Apr 1845
GRIFFITH, Dorcas (Asa) of St. Charles
                   By Rev. George Smith

ROBINSON, William G. 23 August   SPRIG 1 Sep 1849
ISBELL, Elizabeth (William)   Rev. William Tatum
          "All of Greene Co." Her name is shown as
                Barbey E. in published records.

ROBNETT, Samuel F.   9 June   PAMJ 11 Jun 1836
RITCHEY, Mary (William)   Rev. Fuqua
                   All of Marion Co.
          (She died 27 July 1848 in her 28th year --
                   from a newspaper item.)

ROHRER, J. W. , MD   11 March   NERA 15 Mar 1849
MATTHEWS, Emma S. (William T.) Rev. J. M. Peck
                   All of St. Louis.

ROSS, Washington, of KY   "Tuesday last"   COP 3 Mar 1842
JANUARY, Eliza (Peter) of Boone Co.   Rev. Isaac Jones
                (Jones was a Presbyterian minister.)

ROUSE, Jacob of Monroe Co.   no date shown   HAJ 25 Nov 1847
ROUSE, Polly of Ralls Co.   Rev. Allen Rouse
          Bridesmaid, Ann Rouse; best man, John Rouse.

ROWLAND, Finis E.   12 March   COP 9 Apr 1842
SHOOK, Zerelda Ann (David) Rev. George M. Effinger

RUCKER, Dr. Angus A. "Thursday week"   BRUNS 1 Jun 1841
FRY, Leah W., granddaughter of John W. Fry
          "All of Howard Co." No minister or J.P. shown.

RUGGLES, Levi   13 April   LADB 24 Apr 1848
BAIRD, Mrs. C. M.   Rev. George W. Fenton
                   All of Louisiana, Pike Co. MO

RULE, Alexander Scott   5 November   SLDU 7 Nov 1846
CARTER, Virginia Ann, formerly of Richmond VA.
                   By Rev. Richard Mawdsley
          (Rule was a son of William K. & Nancy Faris Rule.
          He died 26 April 1854, ae 29y 8m.)

RUNNELS, Lorenzo   "Thursday evening last"   COP 18 Dec 1841
SUTTON, Mary Ann (B. F.)   Rev. George M. Effinger

RUSSELL, Joseph William, Esq., of St. Louis   MORE 16 Nov 1843
FRIZZELL, Mary Langdon, granddaughter of the late
          Col. George Bollinger in Cape Girardeau
                   By Rev. Rice, no date.

RUTHERFORD, James   9 March   LADB 13 Mar 1848
VANNOY, Margaret Ann (Nathan)   Elder Greenup Jackman
                    All of Pike Co.

SAMPSON, John 17 November   COP 25 Nov 1842
WOODS, Martha J. (Michael, deceased) Rev. McAfee
                    All of Boone Co.

SAMPSON, John B.   18 April   MORE 6 May 1850
GREEN, Mrs. Emma   Rev. Jeter

SAMPSON, Major Thomas L.   in Rocheport 2 November   MORE 11 Nov 1848
MELODY, Jessie B. (only dau/G.H.C., of St. Louis)
                    By Rev. Coalter

SAPPINGTON, James   21 May   MOAR 26 May &
PIPKIN, Tibitha (Col. Philip)   Rev. J. Kennedy   3 Jun 1840
                    "Both of Gravois."

SAPPINGTON, John M.   20 March   SLOB 27 Mar 1834
PIPKIN, Emeline (Col. Philip)   Rev. Robert Renick

SAPPINGTON, William J. of St. Louis Co. 2 April   NERA 15 Apr 1845
BAKER, Rachel (John)   Rev. Walker D. Shumate

SATTERLEE, Dr. Benedict of Elmira NY   SLOB 3 Mar 1836
MATHER, Martha Ann of Fairfield, Herkimer Co. NY
                    By Rev. David Chassell
          "Dr. S. and lady are destined for the Pawnee Mission
          and expect to leave Ithaca NY March 1 with four other
          individuals to go to their stations near Platte
          River, Missouri Territory."

SAUNDERS, Dr. R. H., of Glasgow no date shown   BOLT 21 Aug 1841
HUGHES, Mary Eliza (Rowland) no minister or J.P. shown

SAUSSER, William, of Hannibal "last evening"   HAG 24 Dec 1846
FUQUA, Adelaide (M.) of Mason Twp. Rev. Thomas Lea

SAVAGE, Rev. F. A. of Glasgow   no date shown   MODE 1 Dec-
PULLIAM, Caroline T. (Drury) of Saline Co.   29 Nov 1847
                    No minister or J. P. shown.

SCHOEFFLER, Charles C., of St. Louis in Hennepin IL   NERA 14 Jun 1849
SAUER, Louisa, of St. Louis   Rev. Dickey, 11 June

SCHROTER, George   4 January in Ralls Co.   PWH 20 Jan 1844
GERARD, Agnes (William, of Ralls Co.) Rev. Wm. P. Cochran

SCOTT, Alex S.   18 May in Montgomery Co.   NERA 26 May 1845
DELANEY, Emily (county records were destroyed)

SCOTT, George W. "Thursday last"   COP 4 Dec 1841
OLDHAM, Sarah S. (William) Rev. Isaac Jones, Presbyterian
                    All of Boone Co.

SCOTT, R. E.   20 December   COP 25 Dec 1841
OLDHAM, Ann H. (William B.) Rev. Isaac Jones, Presbyterian

SCOTT, Samuel, a printer   8 January   FAME 16 Jan 1834
CLEAVELAND, Mrs. Elizabeth, of Edwardsville IL
                    By Rev. Schon

SCOTT, William   "Thursday evening last"   JEFRE 27 Jun 1835
DIXON, Elizabeth (Henry)   Rev. McAfee

SCOTT, William P.   4 December   NERA 5 Dec 1845
HALL, Martha (Charles R.)   Rev. Potts

SCUDDER, Capt. John, late of Cincinnati   FAME 28 Aug 1834
PERRINE, Rebecca (2nd dau/Matthew, of Monmouth Co. NJ)
      Saturday evening by Rev. Potts.

SCUDDER, John, of Birmingham MO in Randolph Co. IL   NERA 24 Jul 1845
MONTFORD, Julia, formerly of Philadelphia 15 July
      By Rev. Mitchell at the home of Samuel E. Clement.

SELMES, T. R. of Hannibal in Christ Church, St. Louis   HWU 14 Nov 1850
BENTON, Sarah P. of Vergennes VT   8 November
      By Bishop Hawks

SELTZER, Daniel C. 3 December in Marion Co.   PWH 12 Dec 1840
WILLIAMSON, Sarah (Robert)   Rev. Tucker
      "her parents consenting"

SETTLE, A. F.   14 December   MODE 5 Jan 1848
TURNER, Tabitha Ann (James Jr.) no minister or J.P. shown

SHACKELFORD, E. D., MD "Tuesday"   MODE 12/10 May 1847
BULL, Henrietta V. (John) no minister or J.P. shown

SHADINGER, Mike, of Fayette 4 February   COMB 11 Feb 1847
RIDER, Mrs. Crescience, of Cooper Co. John Garnett, Esq.
      At the home of John Dahrman.

SHAMP, H. S.   10 April   CANE 18 Apr 1850
DEAN, Mrs. Hannah J.   Rev. E. M. Marvin

SHANDS, Joseph G.   "Tuesday"   MOSN 5 Jan 1839
WALTON, Clarissa (youngest dau/Joseph) Rev. Elliott?
      (Probably should be Rev. Eliot?)

SHARP, Leonard B. 25 February in Benton Co.   WARV 3 Mar 1849
GIBSON, Nancy (eldest dau/Hawkins M.) Elder M. Gray

SHAW, George D.   7 June   BEA 23 Jun 1831
WALTON, Mary (George)   Joel Musick
      At George Walton's farm in St. Louis Co.

SHAW, John, formerly of Washington City 14 February   MORE 28 Feb 1832
HOOD, Jane (William)   Rev. Chamberlain

SHAW, Williamson   12 November   LADB 23 Nov 1846
SHAW, Martha A. V. (William deceased) Rev. Wm. Barnett
      All of Pike Co.

SHELBY, Richard P. of Saline Co. 6 June   COP 12 Jun 1841
MITCHELL, Mrs. Rebecca (Thomas L. Williams, of
                              Knoxville, TN)
      In Saline Co., by Rev. Dodd.

SHEPPARD, Jeremiah   27 July in Audrain Co.   JEM 17 Aug 1847
DOLLINS, Mary Jane (Richard)   Rev. R. C. Mansfield

SNELL, Maj. Willis W.   1 August   JEM 17 Aug 1847
PLEDG, Susan (W.)   Rev. Nicholas

SNOW, Rev. D. J., Editor of the Illinois <u>Organ</u>   MORE 29 Apr 1850
ROUNDTREE, Lula Harrison (Hon. Hiram) of Hillsboro
              9 April, in Hillsboro, by the Rev. E. Wentworth,
                 President of McKendree College.

SPENCER, Elias, of St. Louis in New Orleans 13 February MORE 22 Feb 1850
COOK, Sarah, formerly of Washington D.C.
                    By Rev. Charles Doughty

SPOONER, George W., of St. Louis in Howard Co.   MORE 17 Jan 1838
PIPES, Georgiana Rhoberta (Patsy)
                In Fayette by Rev. H. L. Boon, no date.

SPRINKLE, David A.   5 December   HAJ 7 Dec 1848
CHURCH, Emily Jane, late of Aberdeen, Brown Co. OH
              By Rev. George C. Light, at the home of
                               John L. Lacy.

SPROUL, Dr. Samuel M. 19 June on Soda Lake, Texas   SPRIG 28 Jul 1849
CAMPBELL, Mary F. (Maj. John) formerly of Springfield
                    By Rev. Marvin Rogers

STAPLES, John T.   25 August   CANE 30 Aug 1849
WILLIAMS, Mrs. Louisa of Lewis Co. Rev. D. T. Wainwright

STAPLETON, Harrison   in Howard Co., no date shown BOLT 12 Dec 1840
BLYTHE, Mary (Samuel)   Rev. Hampton Boon

STARK, Thomas, of Boonville in Callaway Co.   COMB 22 Oct 1847
RILEY, Eliza Jane (Samuel)   6 October
                    No minister or J. P. shown.

STEEL (SKEEL?) Charles in Hannibal 7 March   BRUNS 31 Mar 1849
MARR, Mary M. (Henry, deceased)
                    No minister or J. P. shown.

STEEN, Alexander of the US Army 17 April   SLDU 29 Apr 1848
MORRISON, Georgiana Antoinette (Maj. P., US Army)
              At Jefferson Barracks by Fr. Bourlandi.

STERNE, J. Y.   20 November in Chariton   MIN 9 Dec 1825
COLLINS, Frances (Col. James)   Rev. John Bull

STEWART, Thomas B. of New Orleans 1 May   JEM 9 May 1848
MARTIN, Mrs. Jane of Cole Co.   William Kerr

STEWART, Dr. William   20 December   LADB 31 Dec 1849
MORRIS, Lydia Jane (2nd dau/Charles R.) Elder Mitchell
                    All of Lincoln Co.

STIRMAN, John J., of Fayetteville AR   13 January   PWH 15 Jan 1842
WINLOCK, Magdalen (George) no minister or J.P. shown

STONE, Caleb Sr.   2 December in Boone Co.   MIN 4 Dec 1830
WOODS, Mary G. (2nd dau/Rev. Anderson) Ebenezer Rodgers

STONE, James   13 October   LADB 18 Oct 1847
YOUNG, Eliza (George)   Elder Greenup Jackman
                    All of Louisiana MO.

STONE, Judge John C. 22 October in Henry Co.   JEM 17 Nov 1846
SMITH, Margaret Ann (James)   Rev. A. Jones
                    All of Henry Co.

STONER, Isaac, of St. Louis in Franklin Co. no date   MORE 30 Jan 1836
ROBERTS, Mrs. Nancy L., formerly of Clarke Co. VA
               At Union; no minister or J. P. shown.

STORY, Stephen   5 February   STGAZ 20 Feb 1846
ROBIDOUX, Mrs. Betsy   Samuel C. Hall
                    All of St. Joseph.

STOVER, Elisha B. in Marion Co. 23 February   PWH 5 Mar 1842
McMURRY, Emily Jane (William) Rev. Richard Sharp

STOVER, Levi   31 December   LEXP 7 Jan 1845
DAILY, Mrs. Elizabeth   A. W. Henning, Esq.

STUCKER, Elisha B., of Portland, Callaway Co.   MODE 27/25 Oct 1847
HERNDON, Agnes E. (James Esq. of "Missouri House")
          In Jefferson City 14 October, no minister
                    or J. P. shown.

SUBLETT, Col. P. B.   16 February in Lewis Co.   PWH 26 Feb 1842
STEPHENS, Mary Ann (John)   Rev. Lillard

SULLIVAN, Thomas   "Monday"   BRUNS 23 Dec 1848
ANDERSON, Jane Virginia (David) all of Chariton Co.
               No minister or J. P. shown.

SWEARINGEN, James   "Tuesday"   SLOB 16 Jan 1834
FARRAR, Martha (Dr. B. G.)   Rev. Schon

SWEREINGEN, James T. "Tuesday evening last"   JEFRE 7 Sep 1839
SCRUGGS, Susan Ann (James)   William M. Kerr

SWITZLER, William F.   29 August   MORE 6 Sep 1843
ROYALL, Mary Jane (J. B.)   Rev. Isaac Jones
                    All of Columbia.

SWOPE, Samuel S.   5 October   MODE 13/11 Oct 1847
EDWARDS, Martha O. (Capt. C.) no minister or J.P. shown

SYKES, James Jr.   16 February   SLDU 18 Feb 1847
PRESBURY, Martha (George C., formerly of Baltimore.)
                    By Bishop Hawkes

TATE, Andrew   in Marion Co. 21 December   PWH 23 Dec 1843
PRAY, Sarah (Stephen)   William H. Claggett, Esq.

TATE, Col. C. B., formerly of Hannibal 14 September   HAJ 20 Sep 1849
DAVIS, Mrs. Louisa, widow of Cornelius C., of Monticello
               In Monticello, Lewis Co., by Rev. E. M. Marvin

TATE, Maj. James, of Fulton "Wednesday evening last" JEFRE 24 Apr 1841
LISLE, Sophia D. (Daniel) of KY
          In Jefferson City, no minister or J. P. shown.

TAYLOR, "Old Uncle Harry" in his 65th year   PWH 19 Nov 1842
MAUPIN, Mrs. Sarah, age 37   Rev. J. Lanius

TAYLOR, John H. of Saline Co. in Lafayette Co.   JEM 23 Nov 1848
CAMPBELL, Mary (James)   3 November
                No minister or J. P. shown.

TAYLOR, Townsen S.   in Howard Co. 4 November   COMB 12 Nov 1847
PERRY, Amanda (Thomas)   Rev. Thomas Fristoe

TAYLOR, William B. of Mercer Co. KY   no date   LEXP 26 Nov 1844
BRISCOE, N. E., late of KY   no minister or J.P. shown
                At the home of George B. Warren in Lafayette Co.

TERRELL, Alexander W., of St. Joseph, in Howard Co.   BRUNS 27 Jan 1849
BOULDIN, Anne D. (Capt. James E. of Howard Co.)
                18 January, no minister or J. P. shown.

THAW, John, formerly of Washington City   no date   BEA 23 Feb 1832
HOOD, Jane (late William)   Rev. Hiram Chamberlain
                        "in Boonville"

THOMAS, Dr. James B., formerly of Easton MD 26 August COMB 27 Aug 1846
WALLACE, Lucy J. of Potosi   Rev. William G. Bell
                        "in Boonville"

THOMAS, James S.   "Thursday last"   BEA 2 Jan 1830
SKINNER, Mary Ann (Curtis, a merchant of St. Louis)
                No minister or J. P. shown.

THOMPSON, Capt. Joseph W.   30 December   PWH 1 Jan 1842
BATES, Sarah E. (Moses)   Rev. Dr. Ely

THRASHER, Benjamin   20 April   HAJ 29 Apr 1847
MOSS, Laura J. (Luke, deceased)   Rev. Richard Sharp
                All of Marion Co.

THRASHER, Thomas   in Marion Co. 1 June   PWH 10 Jun 1843
DUCKER, Frances   Rev. Broaddus

THRUSTON, Dr. William of Morgan Co. 16 November   BORE 21 Nov 1843
THRUSTON, Sarah Washington (William) late of SC
                At Versailles, Morgan Co., by E. J. Salmars.
                "Greenville Mountaineer, please copy."

TILDEN, Richard   13 November   NERA 13 Nov 1845
DAVIS, Hannah (Samuel) formerly of MA   Rev. Eliot

TINDLE, Josiah (Joseph?)   "Thursday" in Howard Co.   BOLT 26 Feb 1842
SWITZLER, Caroline (Simeon)   H. L. Boon

TODD, Thomas D. of Andrew Co.   13 October   COP 21 Oct 1842
HELM, Cloe (Charles) of Boone Co. Elder M. P. Wills

TOLSON, B. H.   14 June   BOLT 18 Jun 1842
DOWNING, Eliza Jane (David R.)   Rev. J. P. Lancaster
                "All of this county."

TOMPKINS, Hon. George   "Thursday last"   MIN 11 Sep 1824
LIENTZ, Elizabeth (eldest dau/William) Justice Williams

TORODE, John   13 March   SLOB 27 Mar 1834
HUNTINGTON, Nancy (eldest dau/Jonathan)
                By Rev. Edwin F. Hatfield

TOWNSEND, Jabez R.   20 February in Springfield MO   MORE 8 Apr 1844
CRENSHAW, Susannah S. V. (William T.) late of Nashville
                No minister or J. P. shown.

TRENT, Fred W.   22 August   BRUNS 26 Aug 1848
REDDING, Sarah (I. W.) no minister or J. P. shown
                All of Keytesville.

TRIBBLE, John L., merchant of Spencerburg   LADB 21 Dec 1846
LEACH, Agnes (Dr. F. B.) also of Spencerburg
                17 December by Rev. H. N. Wilber.

TRIMBLE, Dr. B. F. of Missouri 22 April   LADB 24 May 1847
DISHMAN, Catherine B. of Lexington KY   Rev. Brown

TRIPLETT, Elias of Marion Co. in Shelby Co. 10 March   PWH 28 Mar 1840
PARSONS, Jane (David, of Shelby Co.) Rev. Lowthoan?

TRIPLETT, Th. J.   22 September   COP 25 Sep 1841
HITT, Sarah J. (William Y.) Rev. George M. Effinger

TUCKER, Appolinarius of Ste. Genevieve 27 February   MOSN 10 Mar 1838
TAYLOR, Elizabeth Jane (George, of St. Francois Co.)
                By Rev. Odine

TUCKER, Rev. J. T. of the Hannibal Presbyterian Church   NERA 10 Oct 1845
SHACKFORD, Ann D. (John, deceased)   7 October
                By Rev. James Townsend

TUCKER, Nathaniel B. "at Franklin," no date   MIN 4 May 1830
SMITH, Lucy Ann (Gen. T. A.)   Rev. William Redman

TUNE, John H.   3 February   LADB 15 Feb 1847
POWEL, Mrs. Martha Ann of Lincoln Co.
                By Elder A. D. Landram

TURNER, Edward of Fayette Co. KY   7 November   PWH 11 Nov 1843
BRYAN, Sarah T. (Lewis)   Rev. Tucker

TURNER, Flemming   30 March in Marion Co.   PWH 8 Apr 1843
LYELL, Mary M. (John)   Rev. Horace Brown

TURNER, Talton   1 December in Howard Co.   MIN 18 Feb 1820
EARICKSON, Sarah S. (James) late of Jefferson Co. KY
                No minister or J. P. shown.

TURNER, William of Pleasant Mount 12 September   JEM 28 Sep 1847
HARRISON, Martha (J. B.) of Tuscumbia
                In Miller Co., no minister or J. P. shown.

TYREE, A. F. of Lexington "Thursday last"   BRUNS 24 Feb 1848
CHILES, Sarah M. (Walter G., of Glasgow)
                In Howard Co., no minister or J. P. shown.

VANDEVENTER, Rev. J. C. of the MO Annual Conference   LADB 31 Aug 1846
GRIMES, Elizabeth Ann (only dau/Capt. John)
                24 August in Paynesville by Rev. J. Lanius.

VAN DOREN, William   20 May   COP 29 May 1841
BARNETT, Mrs. Mary   Rev. Isaac Jones, Presbyterian

VANOVER, William R. of the Franklin _Independent_   BRUNS 27 Sep 1840
SUTLIFF, Mary M. of Smyrna, NY   5 September
               In Franklin Co., no minister or J. P. shown.

VAUGHN, Dr. I. P. of Glasgow   27 May   BOLT 29 May 1841
WARD, Ann (William) of Howard Co.   H. L. Boon

VIVION, James   27 December in Howard Co.   MIN 4 Jan 1828
BROWN, Mrs. Mary   Ebenezer Rodgers

WADDELL, James, a merchant of St. Louis "Monday last" BEA 27 May 1830
JARROTT, Felicite (youngest dau/N., deceased)
               By Rev. Lutz

WALDEN, Dr. Charles F.   24 June   LADB 4 Jul 1846
CREW, Emily (John)   Rev. James W. Campbell
               All of Pike Co.

WALDEN, James of Randolph Co.   30 April   MODE 13/11 May 1846
DENNY, Amanda J. (J., of Howard Co.)
               By Rev. Samuel Davis

WALES, John of Shelby Co.   11 October   HAJ 18 Oct 1849
LEWIS, Mary P. (eldest dau/John R.) in Hannibal
               By Rev. Lorance

WALKER, Hiram G. 6 June in Moreau Twp.   JEFRE 18 Jun 1833
AMOS, Nancy (Rev. Benjamin)   Rev. Lewis Shelton

WALKER, Robert W. of Jefferson City   20 March   JEFRE 24 Feb 1844
DYER, Margaret (Col. William H.) in Callaway Co.
               By Rev. Goodrich

WALLACE, Benjamin F.   1 August in Monroe Co.   JEM 17 Aug 1847
WILLOCK, Virginia J. (Gen. David, of Palmyra)
               By Rev. John Gallimore

WARE, John H.   24 June   COP 26 Jun 1841
MARNEY, Sarah J. (Amos)   Young Hicks

WARREN, W. H.   "Sunday last"   BRUNS 16 Dec 1847
ROSSMAN, Mrs. Sophia no minister or J. P. shown

WASH, John M. A. 4 June in Lewis Co.   PWH 13 Jun 1840
ADAMS, Mary Ann (Charles, of Lewis Co.)
               By Rev. P. N. Haycraft

WASSON, Lieut. Golden   13 February in Howard Co. BRUNS 24 Feb 1848
PERRIN, Juanna (Charles) no minister or J. P. shown

WATERS, Louis of Orwell OH   1 April   NERA 15 Apr 1845
SAPPINGTON, Frances (John)   Judge Joseph Sale

WATKINS, William S. of Warrenton 27 November   NERA 25 Dec 1845
CUSTER, Arcelia J. (Joseph, late of Troy)
               In Warren Co. by Rev. Jefferson Wright.

WATSON, George J. 23 November in St. Louis Co.   SLDU 24 Nov 1846
O'BRIEN, Ellen, late of Limerick City, Ireland
               By Fr. Wheeler

WATTS, George   in Howard Co. 23 January   MIN 25 Jan 1827
HARDIN, Elizabeth (Judge)   William Taylor

WATTS, John   14 October   LADB 18 Oct 1847
HENDRICK, Martha (eldest dau/Johnson, of Bowling Green)
                By Rev. William F. Watson

WEBB, Frederick F. of St. Louis 14 October   MODE 27/25 Oct 1847
HERNDON, Elizabeth G. (James of "Missouri House")
         At Jefferson City, no minister or J.P. shown.

WEBB, George W.   28 March   HAJ 5 Apr 1849
McDANIEL, Mary E. (William)   Rev. J. L. Bennett
                All of Marion Co.

WELLS, Erastus   7 February   SLINT 11 Feb 1850
HENRY, Isabella (Hon. John, late of Jacksonville IL)
                By Rev. Parks

WELLS, Dr. John C.   22 February   LADB 1 Mar 1847
CUSTER, Catherine (2nd dau/Joseph) Rev. David Dimond
            All of Troy, Lincoln Co.

WERNECK, Nicholas 17 December in Marion Co.   PWH 19 Dec 1840
DRESCHER, Elizabeth (Daniel)   Rev. J. P. Bost
         Bost was Pastor of the German Protestant Church.

WEST, William, MD   21 February   MORE 2 Mar 1847
McCORMACK, Catherine (James, deceased) of Jefferson Co.
                By Rev. George Effinger

WETZELL, William V. of Lexington in Augusta, IL   NERA 25 Nov 1845
SKINNER, Ann Atwood (Alfred) of Augusta IL
            19 November by Rev. W. Griswold

WHALLEY, Christo. 3 September   St. Paul's Church   NERA 8 Sep 1845
WILLIAMS, Emily (R. P.)   Rev. P. R. Minard
                All of St. Louis.

WHITE, Isham   in Marion Co. 9 November   PWH 11 Nov 1843
BAKER, Alcinda (Philip)   Broaddus

WHITE, Robert   3 September   SLDU 7 Sep 1846
WHITE, Isabella (J. H., at his home) Rev. J. Boyle

WHYTE, I. T. of Oregon MO "Sunday evening last"   SJA 29 Nov 1850
PROUTS, Mrs. Sarah, widow of George   in Oregon
                By Rev. Greenberry Tharp

WIGGINS,Samuel B.   Thursday   MOSN 2 Jun 1838
WILSON, Mary (James deceased, of Philadelphia)
                By Rev. A. Bullard

WILBURN, Thomas J. of NY   9 August   JEFRE 15 Aug 1835
GORDON, Elizabeth (Capt. John C.) Rev. Hiram H. Baber

WILCOX, Dr. Daniel P.   no date shown   MIN 23 Jul 1822
MOSS, Eliza (Dr. James W.)   Ezekiel Rodgers
                In Boone Co.

WILCOX, J. B. of Hudson OH   5 December   SLINT 10 Jan 1850
PAPIN, Minnie (Alexander, deceased)   Fr. Dahmer

WILDER, Henry A., formerly of Hingham MA   NERA 17 Oct 1845
LAIDAIN, Mary Ann   13 October by Rev. Holmes

WILKINSON, Jonathan   23 March in Hannibal   HAG 30 Mar 1848
BROWN, Mrs. Violet   Elder D. T. Morton

WILKINSON, Francis H. in Perry Co. 23 January   MORE 1 Feb 1838
BROWN, Julia (Robert T. Sr.)   Rev. Raho

WILKINSON, Walter B.   in Perry Co. 16 August   MORE 20 Aug 1838
PRATT, Emily (Joseph)   Rev. Timon
                    At Pratt's Landing.

WILLARD, P. H. of Chillicothe IL, formerly of
                                Lowell MA   JEFRE 13 May 1844
GOODRICH, Elizabeth of St. Louis,
                    formerly of Pittsfield VT
                5 April by Rev. Goodrich; ceremony
                performed in Jefferson City.

WILLIAMS, John B., formerly of the Liberty Tribune   COMB 25 Sep 1847
KEENE, Elenorah (John G.) 13 September in Boone Co.
                By Rev. A. R. Macy

WILSON, Benjamin, late of Cumberland Co. VA   MORE 24 Jun 1839
BROWN, Mary Speakman (youngest dau/James, of Saline Co.)
                5 June by Rev. Thomas Wallace.

WILSON, John W. of Bolivar, Polk Co. in Cedar Co.   MORE 14 Apr 1847
COWAN, Nancy (George R., of Cedar Co.) 7 April
                By Rev. V. Peutzer

WILSON, Singleton W., attorney   no date   MOSN 26 May 1838
BARR, Mary J. "lately of New York." in St. Louis
                No minister or J. P. shown.

WILSON, William   "Thursday evening last"   MIN 22 Jul 1823
COOLEY, Hannah (Joseph)   George Chapman Esq.
                In Howard Co.

WINSTON, William   "Thursday last"   JEM 16 Nov 1847
DIXON, Catherine (Levi)   Rev. Allen

WISE, Henry J. of St. Louis 21 September   SLDU 23 Sep 1847
WISE, Lavinia (Hon. J. M.) of Greenburgh PA
                By Rev. Lynd

WISE, Dr. W. H. of Louisiana MO   18 July   LADB 14 Aug 1848
OVERALL, Mary A. of Nelson Co. KY   Rev. P. B. Samuels

WOLFF, John   10 February   MOSN 17 Feb 1838
ULRICI, Clara (C.)   Rev. G. Wall

WOODEN, Ransom   19 July   HAJ 26 Jul 1849
PARIS, Jincy W. (John B.) of Ralls Co. John M. Johnson

WOODS, James D.   30 March   COP 2 Apr 1842
WILLIS, Julia A. (Rev. Fielding) Rev. R. S. Thomas
                All of Boone Co.

WOODS, James M.   6 February   CGWE 16 Feb 1849
SLOAN, Margaret C.   "at the home of L. H. Flinn in
        Greenville, all of that place." Rev. Perry

WOODS, Peter   14 December in Howard Co.   MIN 17 Dec 1822
COLLIER, Nancy (eldest dau/Aaron)   Rev Tharp

WOODS, William   "Thursday last"   BOLT 18 Apr 1840
TURNER, Mary Ann (Rev. Lynch)   John Harvey

WOODS, William Shepard of St. Louis   no date   in Potosi MORE 18 Oct 1847
COWAN, Alice (Rev. John F. and Mary E.)
            By Rev. John Cowan

WOODSON, William G.   29 July in Chariton Co.   NERA 7 Aug 1845
COALE, Mrs. Juliet C. no minister or J. P. shown

WRAY, James H.   21 April   LADB 6 May 1850
CROSSMAN, Mrs. Jane   Justice Price

WRIGHT, Charles S.   13 January   HAJ   7 Feb 1850
THURMAN, Rhoda Ann (Jeptha)   Rev. J. A. Light
            All of Marion Co.

WRIGHT, Erie   28 December at the 1st Baptist Church   SLDU 4 Jan 1847
OWEN, Mary Elizabeth (eldest dau/John and Jemima)
            By Rev. Linn

WRIGHT, Leland   6 October in Fayette   PWH 23 Oct 1841
HUGHES, Catherine (Mrs. Nancy)   Elder A. M. Lewis

YATES, John, a merchant "recently" in Fulton   MORE 27 May 1828
NICHOLS, Ann (George) no minister or J. P. shown

YOUNG, John A. of Louisiana MO   8 June   BGRAD 11 Jun 1842
MANNEN, Mary Ann (Asa, of Montgomery Co.)
            By Walter McQuie

YOUNG, John H. of Cincinnati 29 November   MORE 30 Nov 1849
PERRY, Julia V. (R., Esq., formerly of Schenectady NY)
        At St. George's Church by Rev. E. Carter Hutchinson.

YOUNG, John (son of Lieut. Governor) 22 January   LEXP 28 Jan 1845
BELLES, Nancy B. (Henry)   Rev. W. C. Ligon

ZIEGLER, Conrad C. (Sebastian and Lucy) of
                            Ste. Genevieve   MORE 10 Nov 1840
BOSSIER, Elvina (Gen. J. B.) 29 October
            In Fredericktown, by Rev. Cellini.

ZOTZ, M. Martin   "Thursday week" at Glasgow   BRUNS 18 May 1848
MORRIS, Susan Martha (eldest dau/late Judge)
            No minister or J. P. shown.

                            #

ADAMS, Catherine - Jacob BLOCK
    Mary Ann - John M.A. WASH
    Mary P. - Rev. Leroy D.
        HATCHITT
AILSMAN, Sarah - Woodruff LEE
ALCORN, Jane B. - William SLOAN
ALEXANDER, Mrs. Eliza Jane -
    Col. Thomas NELSON
ALLCORN, Elizabeth - James EVANS
ALLEN, Mrs. Icybindy -
    Horace KINGSBURY
    Louisa - Thomas SMITHER
    Mary - Robert M. ALLEN
    Zerelda - Jos. NICHOLSON
ALLISON, Lucy -
    Capt. Vincent P. JOHNSON
    Selinda - Wm. ADKISSON
ALSOP, Laura - Wm. GLEASON
AMOS, Nancy - Hiram G. WALKER
ANCELL, Gabriella - John DEAN
ANDERSON, Cecelia Sophia -
    Nicholas B. DRAKE
    Jane Virginia -
    Thomas SULLIVAN
ARNOLD, Statira -
    Thornton H. FREEMAN
ASHBY, Eliza J. - Wm. E. LEEPER
ASKINS, Harriet - Abraham BARTON
AUSTIN, Lucy J. -
    Archibald AUSTIN

BACON, Mariette - James COMFORT
BAIRD, Mrs. C.M. - Levi RUGGLES
BAKER, Alcinda - Isham WHITE
    Eliza - David PITTMAN
    Elizabeth -
    Joshua J. CHILDS
    Elizabeth J. -
    John N. CARTER
    Narcissa -
    Dr. James M. COVINGTON
    Rachel - Wm. J. SAPPINGTON
    Sarah Ann - Thomas SMOOT
BARNES, Elender -
    Dr. J. R. DINWIDDIE
BARNETT, Mrs. Mary -
    William VAN DOREN
    Mrs. Mary - Henry OWENS
    Rachel - Andrew KINCAID
BARR, Mary Eliza -
    Middleton B. SINGLETON
    Mary J. - Singleton WILSON

BASYE, Frances W. -
    Ambrose D. REYNOLDS
    Narcissa - A. KING
BATES, Sarah E. -
    Capt. Joseph THOMPSON
BEATY, Mary Ann - B. D. LUCAS
BELL, Martha - Dr. James A. KERR
BELLES, Nancy B. - John YOUNG
BENIGHT, Mary - D. M. FORCE
BENNET, Mary - Thomas NEAL
BENNETT, Elizabeth Ann -
    Alexander S. KENNEDY
BENTON, Sarah -
    Capt. Joshua B. BRANT
    Sarah P. - T. R. SELMES
BERNARD, Frances - James MAJOR
BERRIAN, Catherine W. -
    Thomas INGRAM Sr.
BERRY, Ann - James ARROT
BLACKFORD, Mary Jane -
    Leonard DOBBINS
BLAKEY, Lucinda Ann -
    James L. BENSON
BLOCK, Eliza Ann - Levi T. CARR
BLOW, Martha Ella Taylor -
    Charles D. DRAKE
BLYTHE, Mary - Harrison STAPLETON
BOLAND, Mrs. Catherine -
    William LAWLER
BOLTON, Mary Ann - Wm. P. MABEN
BOSSIER, Elvina -
    Conrad C. ZIEGLER
BOSWELL, Ann Shuter - John PECK
BOTTS, Elizabeth - Stephen SHIPP
BOUCHELLE, Ellena M. -
    Rev. Isaac JONES
BOULDIN, Anne D. -
    Alexander W. TERRELL
BOULWARE, Mrs Sarah -
    Reese DAVIS
BOWEN, Fanny - Coleman BULLARD
BOWEN or Martha J. -
BOWER   Francis HOLLINGSWORTH
BOWER, Mary J. - Barton GRANT
BOYCE, Jane -
    Dr. Alexander MOORE
    Mary E. - Peter PARKER
BOYD, Lucy Ann Rebecca -
    R. C. HENDRICK
BOYER, Alcinda - Dr. A. KERNS
BRADLEY, Mary Ann - M.P. AMSBURY
BRAIL, Mrs. Christina -
    Thomas MOORE

BRANNIN, Ann - Andrew GIPSON
BREADY, Maria - Jacob LITTLETON
BRIGGS, Mary Catherine -
   Anderson JOHNSON
BRISCOE, Mary Jane - Andrew LEMMON
  N. E. - Wm. B. TAYLOR
BRIZENDINE, Mrs. Sarah -
   Dr. Daniel L. DAVIS
BROADWELL, Ann Maria -
   John W. DOUBLEDAY
BROOKS, Amanda - Joseph OWENS
  Louisa - John MITCHELL
BROOKSHIRE, Mrs. Abigail -
   George GREENWAY
BROTHERTON, Mrs. Mary Ann -
   Capt. John ELLIOTT
BROWN, Julia - Francis WILKINSON
  Mrs. Mary - James VIVION
  Mary Speakman -
   Benjamin WILSON
  Pamelia - Henry B. MILLER
  Susan - Jeptha LAKE
  Mrs. Violet -
   Jonathan WILKINSON
BROWNING, Mildred - John M. ELLIS
  Sarah L. - Dr. Wm. J.KNOX
BROYLES, Martha C. -
   Charles S. PIERCE
BRYAN, Mrs. Mary - Thomas NESBIT
  Sarah T. - Edward TURNER
BRYANT, Martha - James C. GILLUM
BUCHANAN, Sallie -
   Dr. Wm. M. McPHEETERS
BUCHHOLTZ, Mrs. Catherine -
   Jacob P. MAUZE
BUCKNER, Anna W. - Maj. T.M. ADAMS
  Mrs. Susan F. -
   James JAMESON
BULL, Henrietta - E.D. SHACKELFORD
BULLOCK, Mary C. - G. C. JONES
BUNN, Mrs. Sarah - John HOWELL
BURCH, Mary Ann - G. P. GORDON
BURCKHARTT, Elizabeth -
   Samuel G. POTEET
BURD, Martha J.O. - Tho. A. LEWIS
BURGESS, Mary T. - Peter BURNS Jr.
BURKS, Martha Ann Elizabeth -
   John M. FEAZEL
BURNS, Susan E. - Samuel HOFFMAN
BUSH, Elizabeth I. -
   James G. McWILLIAMS
BUTLER, Mary A. V. -
   Thomas T. ELLIOTT

BYRD, Nancy - Edward B. KELSO
CABELL, Pocahontas - A. JOHNSON
CALDWELL, Grizella S. -
   James H. COOK, MD
CALLAHAN, Mrs. Henrietta S. -
   William D. KERR
  Jane B. -
   Lt. F. S. MUMFORD
CALLAWAY, Harriet - Robert CARSON
CAMP, Martha Emily -
   James C. DYER
CAMPBELL, Mary - John H. TAYLOR
  Mary F. -
   Dr. Samuel SPROUL
  Nancy K. - David BELL
CANNON, Caroline E. -
   Elias N. EUBANK
CARMAN, America - Wm. DEARING
CARNEGY, Matilda Louise -
   Barnabas B. KING
CARSON, Mrs. Rebecca -
   Joseph MARTIN
CARTER, Virginia Ann -
   Alexander Scott RULE
CASEY, Catherine - John CLANCY
CASTELLE, Mary - Charles SMITH
CHENIE, Athanlie - Joseph PEASE
CHILES, Sarah M. - A. F. TYREE
CHRISTY, Neville - J.D. JOHNSTON
CHURCH, Emily Jane -
   David A. SPRINKLE
CLARK, Mrs. E.W. - Joseph ECHERT
  Patsey - Jubal HURT
  Precilla A. S. -
   Rev. Samuel H. FORD
  Mrs. Susan - Hugh CRAWFORD
  Mrs. V. G. -
   Smith McGINNIS
CLATWORTHY, Mrs. Mary -
   John CLATWORTHY
CLEAVELAND, Mrs. Elizabeth -
   Samuel Scott
  Lucy P. -
   George SHERRICK
CLENDENIN, Mildred Ann -
   Thomas COURTENAY
CLEVELAND, Juliet Maria -
   Dr. Loring H. REYNOLDS
CLIFFORD, Mrs. Joanna L. -
   Andrew J. BUTLER
COALE, Mrs. Juliet C. -
   William WOODSON

COCHRAN, Sophia P. -
    Malcolm A. LINDLEY
COLLIER, Nancy - Peter WOODS
COLLINS, Mrs. Elizabeth -
    Dr. B. GILLETT
    Frances - J. Y. STERNE
    Mrs. Sarah J. -
    Dr. H. M. PARRISH
CONDON, Elizabeth - Chas. LADEW
CONINGHAM, Jane H.-Wm. H. RAY
COOK, Sarah - Elias SPENCER
COOLEY, Hannah - William WILSON
COPPITT, Mary E. - James HAWKINS
CORDER, Mary Virginia -
    Andrew T. C. GLICK
CORN, Nancy - Thomas BRIDGES
COWAN, Alice - Wm. Shepard WOODS
    Mary Ann -
    Maj. Stephen BATES
    Nancy - John W. WILSON
COWDEN, Jane - Stephen GOLDEN
COX, Cora - Francois PRATTE
    Sarah M. - E. M. MOFFETT
CRAFT, Sarah - James R. DOBYNS
CRANE, Mildred Ann -
    E. T. W. PEGRAM
    Mrs. Sarah Sophronia -
    William M. BARBER
CRENSHAW, Susannah S. V. -
    Jabez R. TOWNSEND
CREW, Emily - Dr. Charles WALDEN
CRIGLER, Elizabeth - Joseph PAGE
CRIGLAR Jemima - John MORIN
    Sarah Ann - John N. KRING
CROSSMAN, Mrs. Jane - James WRAY
CROW, Elouise - Nelson MOORE
CUNNINGHAM, Sarah - Jos. HOWARD
CUSTER, Arcelia J. - Wm. WATKINS
    Catherine -
    Dr. John C. WELLS

DAGUET, Maria Louisa - Wm. GIBSON
DAILY, Mrs. Elizabeth - Levi STOVER
DALE, Sarah F. - Lucian EASTIN Jr.
DALEY, Sarah - F. B. BRIGGS
DALY, Elizabeth - Samuel C. MAJOR
DARR, Mrs. Emily -
    Allen B. McDONALD
DAUGERTY, Elizabeth - James SMITH
DAVIDSON, Rebecca -
    Capt. Amos BRUCE
DAVIS, Hannah - Richard TILDEN
    Jane - Hampton LOOKER
    Mrs. Jane E. - John M. DUNCAN

DAVIS, Mrs. Louisa -
    Col. C. B. TATE
    Mary C. E. -
    John B. MASSEY
DEAN, Mrs. Hannah J. -
    H. S. SHAMP
DEFORD, Martha A. -
    Lemuel J. RITCHEY
DELANEY, Emily - Alex S. SCOTT
DE LA PORTE, Theodora -
    Amos COTTING Jr.
DELLINGER, Ellen - Jos. HIGGINS
DENNY, Amanda J. - James WALDEN
DISHMAN, Catherine B. -
    Dr. B. F. TRIMBLE
DIXON, Catherine - Wm. WINSTON
    Elizabeth - Wm. SCOTT
    Lydia - Dr. P.P. FULKERSON
    M. A. - Dr. Geo. LANSDOWN
DOLLINS, Mary Jane -
    Jeremiah SHEPPARD
DONNELLY, Mary A. - D.B. HEALY
DONOHUE, Susan M. - L.F. HAYDEN
DORSEY, Comfort -
    Porter GILCHRIST
DOUGLASS, Margaret - Allen RAINS
DOWNING, Eliza Jane -
    B. H. TOLSON
DRAPER, Julia Ann - W.O. SIMMONS
    Maria - Geo. H. JONES
DRESCHER, Ann Maria -
    Benjamin SLUSS
    Elizabeth -
    Nicholas WERNECK
DUBREVILLE, Olympe - John NEWMAN
DUCKER, Frances - Thos. THRASHER
DUDGEON, Margaret -
    Dr. D. P. NELSON
DUDLEY, Martha - Jacob GEIGER
    Mary A. C. -
    Oliver HARRIS
DUDSON, Mrs. Sarah -
    Andrew J. DAWSON
DUNCAN, Harriet Elizabeth -
    Allen HAMMOND
    Mrs. Susan A. -
    Capt. Nathan MASSEY
DUNKLIN, Emilie S. -
    Faulkland MARTIN
DUNN, Elizabeth - James DUNN
DUPRE, Fanny - George W. LYNCH
DURKEE, Amanthis -
    Henry DEVILBUS

49

DURRETT, Mary T. -
        Henry H. GOODWIN
DUVALL, Mary P. - J. H. McKENNY
DYER, Margaret - Robert W. WALKER

EARHART, Maria Louise -
        Gershon F. DRAKE
EARICKSON, Sarah S. -
        Talton TURNER
EASBY, Cecelia J. - George HYDE
ECKLER, Mrs. F. S. - James MARTIN
EDDY, Elvira Lavinia -
        Lewis W. SMALLWOOD
EDWARDS, Martha O. - Samuel SWOPE
      Sarah O. M. -
        Albert POWELL
ELLIOTT, Mrs. M. A. - John F. BATES
ELY, Mary Ann Miles -
        James H. PATTERSON
ELLIS, Eliza T. - W. E. CLARK
ENGLISH, Mary Catherine -
        John O'NEIL
ESCHENBURG, Jane - H. GALLAGHER
EVANS, Mrs. E. J. - C. B. HOUTS
      Mary - James B. GREEN
EVERETT, Susan J. - Wm. M. BROWN
EWING, Martha Jane - Dr. Geo. DEWEY
      Mary A. -
        Archibald KAVANAUGH
      Pamela M. - Charles BOWMAN

FARLEY, Mrs. Ann M. F. -
        John M. CANNON
FARRAR, Martha - James SWEARINGEN
FERGUSON, Louisa - John B. CLARK
      Sarah - Dr. Robert BELL
FERRELL, Nancy E. -
        John Smith SLADE
FERRIOT, Mrs. Sarah H. -
        Charles R. MUGGAH
FINLEY, Hadassas -
        Alexander H. HENDERSON
FITZHUGH, Lucy Ann - Henry S. COXE
FLINT, Mary - William FUNK
FORBES, Hannah - George HUNTINGTON
FORD, Mrs. Matilda - Wm. MASSEY
FOSTER, Mrs. Mary - John EVANS
      Octavia - Dr. Philip REILY
      Rhoda Ann -
        William Henry BLACKBURN
FRASIER, Therese - John H. CHAFEY
FRAZIER, Mrs. Kezia - Harvey or
        Harry N. COLGAN
FREELAND, Deborah - John H. CURD

FRISTOE, Mary Jane -
        Aaron JENKINS
      Susan Martha -
        Jordan BENTLY
FRIZZELL, Mary Langdon -
        Joseph Wm. RUSSELL
FRY, Leah - Dr. Angus A. RUCKER
FRYER, Caroline - James LINDSAY
FUGATE, Nancy Ann -
        Tandy HUGHES
FULKERSON, Margaret -
        Thomas B. GORDON
FUQUA, Adelaide - Wm. SAUSSER

GARLAND, Mary L. -
        Timothy PAPIN
GARRETT, Mrs. Mary -
        Frederick EHRMIN
GAW, Barbara Ann - James BOGGS
GEARHART, Elizabeth -
        William J. SMITH
GEIGER, Harriet -
        J. M. Fischel GALLATIN
GERARD, Agnes - George SCHROTER
GIBSON, Eliza J. - Geo. DILLARD
      Nancy - Leonard SHARP
      Zerelda Ann -
        James BRADLEY
GILES, Alice - Benjamin BERCIER
GLENN, Julia Ann -
        Shelton B. FARTHING
GOOCH, Mary L. - J. J. GIERS
GOOD, Sarah - J. L. MINOR
GOODMAN, Polly - Thomas F. BAKER
GOODRICH, Elizabeth -
        P. H. WILLARD
GORDEN, Sarah - Chas. MEREDITH
GORDON, Mrs. Eliza M. -
        David RIGBY
      Elizabeth -
        Thomas J. WILBURN
      Elizabeth - Charles
        LAREW or LADEW
GORE, Margaret A. - Wm. HOWELL
GOWER, Anna -
        Dr. H. J. B. McKELLOPS
GRAVES, Elizabeth - Jas. LEEPER
GRAY, Mrs. Elizabeth -
        Augustine BYRAM
GREEN, Mrs. Emma - John SAMPSON
GREGORY, Mary N. -
        Elisha B. JEFFRIES
GRIFFITH, Dorcas -
        John W. ROBINSON

GRIMES, Elizabeth Ann -
        Rev. J. C. VANDEVENTER
        Louisiana - Walter PERKINS
GRISWOLD, Mrs. Anna Adelia -
        Rev. Hiram CHAMBERLAIN
GUELBERTH, Zelina - MATHEW LEGG(S)
GUNN, Abby H. - William CROWELL

HALBERT, Elizabeth Ann -
        Francis DWYER
HALE, Eglantine - Wm. B. GRAVES
        Margaret - Abram SMITH
HALL, Charlotte - Robert P. HALL
      Martha - William P. SCOTT
      Minerva - Henry CHAPELL
HARDIMAN, Leona - R. L. CORDELL
        Mrs. Nancy - Jas. DUNNICA
HARDIN, Elizabeth - George WATTS
        Mary E. - Dr. R. H. SMITH
HARMON, Caroline T. - Taylor BERRY
HARRIS, Eliza - James McCOMAC
      Susan - John JAMESON
      Sarah - GEORGE W. HUNT
HARRISON, Ann Eliza -
* *   Col. G. H. NETHERTON
      Martha J. - Wm. TURNER
      Mary Eliza - Hiram BIGGER
HART, Martha Ann - Thomas HATCHER
      Mrs. Sarah - Willis G. BERRY
HARTLY, Mrs. Frances -
        Horatio JAMESON
HARTT, Sarah - Dr. Thomas PARKS
HAWKEN, Anna Maria - Wm. F. KELLY
HAWKINS, Elizabeth -
        Andrew Jackson McQUITTY
HAYDEN, Martha - J. C. HAMILTON
HAYDON, Rebecca - Arthur DENT
* *
HARRISON, Jane Caroline -
        Fountain M. DUNNICA
* *
HEADRICK, Mary - Robert BOHANNON
HEATH, Jane Lee - Geo. HENDERSON
HELM, Cloe - Thomas D. TODD
HENDERSON, Mrs. C. F. -
        Dr. P. T. DIMMITT
      Eliza M. - Dr. W.B. GORDON
HENDRICK, Martha - John WATTS
HENDRICKS, Nancy - James MOSELY
HENNEGAR, Mrs. Rebecca -
        Alfred J. HAWKINS
HENRY, Angeline - S. W. FINLEY
      Isabella - Erastus WELLS

HENSEY, Catherine Jane -
        Hiram B. BASCOM
HERD, Jane - C. Erwin MOONYHAM
HERNDON, Agnes E. -
        Elisha B. STUCKER
     Elizabeth G. -
        Frederick WEBB
HERYFORD, Missouri -
        Larz ANDERSON
HICKMAN, Mrs. Sophia -
        David LAMME
HILL, Eliza Ann - John W. SMITH
     Eliza Ann - Col. J.F. ALLEN
     Mary - Dr. Eli PENNY
     Nancy Jane - Harvey ARNOLD
HITT, Sarah J. - Th. J. TRIPLETT
HOCKENSMITH, Anna -
        Matthew FLOURNOY
HODGE, Mary - T. J. BALLARD
HOLDEN, Mary Elizabeth -
        Robert T. BROWN Jr.
HOLLMAN, Emily - James Lewis
HOLMAN, Mrs. Caroline Scott -
        George COFFMAN
HOOD, Jane - John THAW or SHAW
HOPE, Margaret M. - J.H. NEELY
HOPSON, Mrs. S. J. - Robt FIFE
HOUGH, Kate - George APPLETON
HOUSTON, Arabella - Thos. HINKLE
HOYLE, Hannah - John W. CLEGHORN
      Hannah - T. P. CUBBERLY
HOYT, Sarah P. - George G. MAHAN
HUGHES, Catherine -
        Leland WRIGHT
     Louisiana -
        John CLEVELAND
     Mary Eliza -
        Dr. R. H. SAUNDERS
     Mary I. - John MORRIS
HULETT, Mrs. Mary J. - J.R. PILE
HUMPHREYS, Sarah Ann -
        Walter RANSOM
HUNTINGTON, Nancy - John TORODE
HUNTSBERRY, Mary Ann Amanda -
        Maj. John C. BLAKEY
HURT, Mary Jane - James FORBIS

IRWIN, Harriet - Moses FUQUA
ISBELL, Elizabeth -
        Wm. G. ROBINSON

JACKSON, Attilla - Geo. BARNARD
     Minerva -
        Alfred M. MORRISON

JAMISON, Elizabeth Jane - Wm. COLE
JANUARY, Eliza - Washington ROSS
JARROTT, Felicite - James WADDELL
JENNINGS, Mary Frances -
                    B. B. DAYTON
JEFFREYS, Ellen Frances -
              Samuel G. LEEPER
JOHNSON, A. M. - Capt. M.M. CLARK
         Ann Elizabeth -
                 Josiah HAINES
         Eugenia Mary Josephine -
              P. M. FORTIER
         Mary A.J. - Joseph C. RAY
         Nancy - John M. PIERCE
         Rosella - Edgar GLEIM
         Mrs. Ruth - Wm. S. JOHNSON
JOHNSTON, Mrs. Catherine -
              Spencer ALEXANDER
         Mary Jane - Joseph HAMILL
JONES, Mrs. Madaline - J.B. JESSUP
       Mrs. Margaret J. -
                 Andrew CAMPBELL
       Mary A. - Wm. G. DOWNING
JORDAN, Sarah - I. F. BENNING

KEENE, Elenorah - John B. WILLIAMS
KEHR, Jane (- Charles C. EITZEN
KELLY, Annie F. - Charles HENDRY
KELSAY, Juliet - Daniel M. LEET
KERR, Agnes E. - Allen RAMSEY
KING, Matilda - Ambrose LYTHE
KIRBY, Jenetta S. -
              Dr. John W. ROBERTS
KNOTT, Mary Ann - John SMITH

LAFON, L. C. - Dr. W. ELLERY
LAIDAIN, Mary Ann - Henry A. WILDER
LANGHAM, Wenona - R. M. BARCLAY
LEACH, Agnes - John L. TRIBBLE
LEAMAN, Eliza J. - John J. BROWN
LeCLAIRE, Theresa M. -
              Col. Amos BRUCE
LEE, Catherine - R. S. JOHNSON
LEITENDORFER, Emilie -
              Samual B. FITHIAN
LEMOINE, Mary Good - Robert NISBET
LENOIR, Julia E. - Samuel CHURCH
LETTON, Lavina Campbell -
              David A. GRAVES
LEWIS, Mrs. Adaline - J.N. ALFORD
       Agnes W. - John GRAVES
       Frances - William HOKE
       Mrs. Mary - Benjamin PYATT
       Mary Frances - C. B. BIOREN
       Mary P. - John WALES

LEWIS, Sarah Jane -
       Dr. H. Walker BRUNS
       Susan M. -
          Col. N. P. MINOR
       Viena - Arguyle BUCHANAN
       Mrs. Virginia -
          Frederick E. BRUNS
       Virginia or Julia -
          Thomas P. SMITH
LIENTZ, Elizabeth - Geo. TOMPKINS
LIONBERGER, Mary Elizabeth -
              J. C. RICHARDSON
LISLE, Sophia D. -
              Maj. James TATE
LITTLE, Ann Elizabeth -
              Edward CLAPP
LITTLEPAGE, Mrs. Nancy -
                 James DICKSON
LITTRELL, Elizabeth - Seth BOTTS
LUCE, Marian B. - E. C. MURRAY
LUCK, Mildred - William PEAY
LUNCY, Zerella - Wm. D. FERGUSON
LYELL, Mary M. - Flemming TURNER

McAFEE, Mrs. Mary E. -
              J. M. DUNCAN
McBRIDE, Eliza Jane -
              Dr. J. K. McBRIDE
McCLELLAND, Olivia -
              Col. John BENT
McCLURE, Ann Rebecca -
              James A. ELDER
McCORMACK, Catherine -
              Dr. William WEST
McCORMIC, Candace - Warren REED
McCORMICK, Amanda Adeline -
              Joseph F. LEWIS
McCOY, Anna J. - William DICKEY
McCRACKEN, Charlotte Anna -
              Henry C. COFFMAN
McCUNE, Mrs. Martha C. -
              Newton McDANNOLD
McDANIEL, Martha Jane -
              William S. PERRY
              Mary E. - Geo. WEBB
McDANIELL, Frances E. -
              Dr. Benjamin BURCH
McDONALD, Mrs. Maria -
              Wm. B. RICHARDSON
McDOWEL, Margaret -
              Col. Ephraim JENKINS
McGOWAN, Sarah - Michael REILLY
McILVAINE, Evaline -
              John Gano BRYAN

52

McKEE, Mrs. Bridget Martha Roy -
    Roderick Charles McKENZIE
McKINNEY, Elizabeth J. -
      Capt. Andrew HENDERSON
      Mrs. Nancy - Chas. CANOLE
McKNIGHT, Asenath - Thomas P. GREEN
McKOIN, Angeline - John HIGHTOWER
McMURRY, Emila Jane - Elisha STOVER
McNAIR, Mary - Dr. John CAMPBELL
McPHERSON, Cornelia - Capt. John
      Thompson DOUGLASS
McQUEEN, Elizabeth Jane -
      Dr. Beverly T. COALTER

MACK, Eliza Jane - Charles ACHLIE
MADDOX, Elizabeth - Dennis ONAN
MAHONY, Frances Ann - Dr. T.M. BACON
MALLORY, Analetta P. -
      Isaac W. McDONALD
      Frances W. - Stephen BYNUM
MALONE, Mrs. Mary -
      Capt. John CAMPBELL
MANN, Phebe - James P. LEWIS
MANNEN, Mary Ann - John A. YOUNG
MARIAR, Mrs. Nancy -
      Sanders BARTLETT
MARKLAND, Eliza Ann - John HARVEY
      Nancy - Ansel GREEN
MARLEY, Nancy - John L. JOHNSON
MARMADUKE, Jane - Levin HARWOOD
MARNEY, Sarah J. - John H. WARE
MARLEY, Mary M. - Charles STEEL
MARSHALL, Mary Ann - Joseph PORTER
MARTIN, Catherine G. - James LITTLE
      Mrs. Jane - Thomas STEWART
      Martha Ann - James KINCAID
      Mary - Henry BATES
MASE, Jemima - Dr. W. W. FREEMAN
MASSIE, Nancy D. - Henry MASSIE
MATHER, Martha Ann -
      Dr. Benedict SATTERLEE
MATSON, Fanny - Capt. N. CAMERON
MATTHEWS, Ann - John W. PAINE
      Emma S. - Dr. J.W. ROHRER
MAUPIN, Mary - James CREWS
      Mrs. Sarah - Harry TAYLOR
MAYO, Mrs. Jane - David PHILLIPPEE
MELODY, Jessie B. -
      Maj. Thomas L. SAMPSON
MILLAN, Ellen - Henry COOK
MILLARD, Mary F. - Asa FARR Jr.
MILLER, Constantia - Wm. L. SMITH
MINOR, Mrs. Eliza - A. H. BUCKNER
MINTER, Helen - George DYE

MITCHELL, Agnes - William MILLER
      Mary - John Henry BROWN
      Mrs. Rebecca -
      Richard P. SHELBY
MOBERLY, Elizabeth -
      James B. GARDNER
MONROE, Margaret R. -
      Capt. E. H. DENNIS
MONTFORD, Julia - John SCUDDER
MOORE, Eliza Jane - Wm. FOWLER
    Helen M. -
      Dr. J. Addison BARRETT
      Margaret - George BARTLEY
MORGAN, Margaret - R. FITZPATRICK
      Mary L. - James BOWLBY
MORRIS, Lydia Jane -
      Dr. William STEWART
      Margaret H. -
      Abraham McPIKE
      Susan Martha -
      M. Martin ZOTZ
MORRISON, Georgiana Antoinette -
      Alexander STEEN
MORROW, Eliza G. - Thos. E. BIRCH
MORTON, Mehitable -
      George P. LAWRENCE
MOSS, Eliza - Dr. Daniel WILCOX
      Laura J. - Benj. THRASHER
      Nancy M. -
      Absalom MEREDITH
MULDROW, Clarinda - Wm. DuBOIS

NALLEY, Mary - Mathew LOFLAND
NEAL, Martha Ann - James E. JONES
NEARNS, Mrs. Mary - Geo. MILLER
NEELY, Letitia C. - Edw. COTTER
NELSON, Mrs. Mary L. -
      H. E. MORELAND
NEWELL, Charlotte - Frederick
      Thomas HARRINGTON
NEWMAN, Henrietta S. -
      Dr. Stuart CALLIHAN
NICHOLS, Ann - John YATES
      Mrs. Sarah - Thos. EMERRY
NOEL, Mary Ellen - Wm. FERRELL
NORTH, Mary E. - James E. ADAMS
NUNNALLY, Mrs. Mary Ann -
      Benjamin SMITH

O'BANNON, Ann J. - M.W. GRISWOLD
O'BRIEN, Ellen - George WATSON
OLDHAM, Ann H. - R. E. SCOTT
      Mrs. Milly - Henry HOLT
      Sarah S. - George SCOTT
OLIVER, Nancy - Samuel CASH

ORR, Mrs. Martha E. - David S. CARY
O'SULLIVAN, Mrs. Ellen -
      Jeremiah O'SULLIVAN
OURY, Elizabeth - Dr. J. T. BELL
OVERALL, Mary A. - Dr. W. H. WISE
OWEN, Mary Elizabeth - Erie WRIGHT
OWENS, Lydia - Samuel DOYAL

PALMER, Elizabeth H. -
      Alfred CHADWICK
PAPIN, Minnie - J. B. WILCOX
PARIS, Jincy W. - Ransom WOODEN
PARKER, Mrs. Joan - Elijah IMPEY
      Lucretia M. - Leazer BLACK
PARKS, Rebecca B. - Jesse DICKSON
PARSONS, Jane - Elias TRIPLET
      Frances - Adam FISHER
PATRICK, Mrs. Ann - Presley HALLEY
PATRIDGE, Charlotte - Louis DOBYNS
PAUL, Mrs. Pembroke -
      Rev. Thomas CAMPBELL
PAXTON, Ann - Dr. F.A.A. HEISEN
PEAKE, Ellen - James DeCAMP
      Susan - Edward McDONNEL
PEARSON, Lavinia -
      Dr. C. M. BRADFORD
PEERY, Amanda - Townsen TAYLOR
PEPPER, Edna - James McCORD
PERREAU, Eleanor - William EARL
PERRIN, Juanna - Lt. Golden WASSON
PERRINE, Rebecca -
      Capt. John SCUDDER
PERRY, Angeline Cornelia -
      Edward BREDELL
      Julia V. - John H. YOUNG
PERSINGER, Sarah Ann -
      James E. JOHNSON
PETERS, Enfield F. - Robt. MILLER
PEYTON, Jane E. - Warren GEORGE
PFOUTS, Mrs. Sarah - I. T. WHYTE
PHILIBERT, Eliza - Andrew BARADA
PIERSON, Elizabeth - Wm. EDDINS
PIPES, Georgiana Rhoberta -
      George W. SPOONER
PIPKIN, Emeline - John M. SAPPINGTON
      Tibitha - James SAPPINGTON
PITTS, Sarah Elizabeth - Wm. R. KIDD
PLEDG, Susan - Maj. Willis W. SNELL
POLLARD, Sarena - Charles HUGHES
PORTER, Mary Haseltine -
      Dr. George H. BOWERS
POTTER, Helen C. -
      Capt. Charles DEAN
POURCILY, Angelique - Richard BARADA

POWEL, Mrs. Martha Ann -
      John H. TUNE
POWELL, Artamesia E. -
      John M. BARTON
PRATTE, Emily - Walter WILKINSON
PRAY, Sarah - Andrew TATE
PRESBURY, Martha - James SYKES Jr.
PRICE, Kate - Lt. Lorin BOSWORTH
      Margaret S. -Daniel GANO
PRIEST, Ann E. - George HAWKINS
PUGH, Joanna - John BRACY
PULLIAM, Caroline T. -
      Rev. F. A. SAVAGE

RAILEY, Pocahontas -
      Joseph V. PARROTT
RAINEY, Cornelia - John FACKLER
RANDOLPH, Susan A. - Andrew
      Jackson KARNEY
RAWLINS, Mary Ann - John MADDOX
RAYNOR, Cornelia - John KING
READ, Mrs. Mary Jane -
      Col. Richard NETHERLAND
REDDING, Sarah - Fred W. TRENT
RENICK, Sarah - Dr. O.F. RENICK
RHOADS, Catherine Ann -
      Johnson HARDWICK
RICHARDSON, Ann Eliza -
      Willard P. HALL
      Delilah -
      John BUNDRIDGE
RICHARTS, Mrs. Mary - Wm. HANNA
RIDER, Mrs. Crescience -
      Mike SHADINGER
RIDGLEY, Hannah - John BROWNLEE
RIGGINS, Mrs. Frances -
      Thomas RECTOR
      Minerva -
      Hardy ROBISON
RIGGS, Avice - Maj. E.H. PERKINS
RILEY, Eliza Jane - Thomas STARK
RITCHEY, Mary - Samuel ROBNETT
ROBERTS, Edwardana -
      Thomas I. EDWARDS
      Mrs. Nancy L. -
      Isaac STONER
ROBERTSON, Mrs. Sophia -
      Edward NENNSTIEL
ROBIDOUX, Mrs. Betsy -
      Stephen STORY
ROBINSON, Ann Elizabeth -
      William HUGHS
RODGERS, Henrietta M. -
      Silas REED

ROGERS, Mrs. Prudence -
    Bishop Jacob CREATH Jr.
   Mrs. Rebecca - John HAMMOND
ROSS, Mrs. Lucretia C. - F.S. PEYTON
   Sarah Jane - William G. FIFE
ROSSMAN, Mrs. Sophia - W.H. WARREN
ROTHWELL, Mary Ann - John P. GIBBS
ROUNDTREE, Lula Harrison -
      Rev. D. J. SNOW
ROUSE, Polly - Jacob ROUSE
   Urania Lowrey - Edw. DRAPER
ROYALL, Mary Jane - Wm. F. SWITZLER
RUCKER, Sarah Ann - John HUTCHESON
RUFF, Sarah Jane - Joseph AMENT
RULAND, Matilda Ann -
    Marcus L. ADDERTON
RUMSEY, Mrs. M. - M. J. MAHAN
RUSSEL, Mrs. Catherine -
    Johnson EVANS
RUSSELL, Elizabeth -
    Dr. Robert P. CHASE
   Elmira or Eleanora -
    Winfield S. HANCOCK

SAMUEL, Mrs. Virginia -
    William PHILLIPS
SAPPINGTON, Anna -Stephen LIGGETT
   Frances - Louis WATERS
   Sarah Ann -
    Joseph FARRELL
SAUER, Louisa - Charles SCHOEFFLER
SAUNDERS, Jane Esther -
   Thomas Ogden DUNCAN
   Nannie J. -Alfred MICHAU
SCOTT, Emily A. - E. H. HUBBARD
   Mrs. Eliza -
   Rev. William P. COCHRAN
   Eliza G. - Byrd LAWLESS
   Mrs. Jane - E. E. CARTER
   Jeannette Elizabeth -
    Richard D. C. SMITH
   Mrs. M. J. - Richard EUBANK
   Martha C. - Noble CUNNINGHAM
   Vesta - John F. NAYLOR
SCRUGGS, Susan Ann -
   James T. SWEREINGEN
SELMES, Sarah Johnson -
   Robert Monroe FUNKHOUSER
SEWARD, Mary C. - Matthew COUDY
SHACKFORD, Ann D. -Rev. J.T. TUCKER
SHANNON, Eliza Maria -
   Samuel Dorrance DIXON
   Laura - Milton BLEDSOE
SHARP, Emily E. - Wm. C. JACKSON

SHAW, Lucy E. -
   Dr. Robert C. PREWITT
  Martha A. V. -
    Williamson SHAW
SHEPPARD, Lucinda A. - Geo. HALE
SHOOK, Zerelda Ann -
   Finis E. ROWLAND
SHROPSHIRE, Susan - Hampton BAKER
SHULSE, Susannah E. -
   Dr. J. H. CRAWFORD
SHURLDS, Josephine - Benj. BATTE
   Mary - George W. DENT
SIMONDS, Jane - Andrew BRACKEN
SIMPSON, Mrs. Mary -
   James L. DOBBIN
SIMS, Mary - Albert BLAIN
SINGLETON, Sarah Frances -
    Edward HOLDEN
SKINNER, Ann Atwood -
    William V. WETZELL
   Jane - E. C. DAVIS
   Mary A. -
   James Nelson BURNES
   Mary Ann - James THOMAS
SLAUGHTER, Caroline E. -
   John L. POINTER
SLOAN, Julia Ann - Samuel A. HILL
   Margaret C. -James WOODS
SMALL, Martha W. - Vines DAVIS
SMITH, Bridget - Peter EARLY
   Catherine - James FOLWELL
   Elizabeth - Wm. SMITH
   Hannah Andromache -
    Charles S. BEARDSLEY
   Harriet - Charles W. HALL
   Lucy Ann -
    Nathaniel B. TUCKER
   Louisa A. - Thomas POWELL
   Margaret Ann -
    Judge John C. STONE
   Martha Ann -
    Samuel HACKLER
   Mrs. Mary Jane -
    Robert Y. SMITH
   Mrs. Mildred -
    Hiram BLACKLEDGE
   Mrs. Susan Caroline -
    F. R. CONWAY
SMOOT, Damarus A. - Andrew BELL
SOAN, Sarah - William P. RIGGINS
SOUTH, Lucy - Hyman BLOCK
SPENCE, Precilla - John T. MARTIN
SPENNY, Mary W. - Wm. H. NORRIS

SPIRES, Jane - R. P. EVANS Jr.
STEPHENS, Mary Ann - Col. P.B. SUBLETT
STEWARD, Ruth - Joseph L. FANT
STEWART, ___ - E. N. JONES
STIBBS, Sarah - Israel LANDIS
STONE, Mary Ann - George CAMPBELL
STOUT, Laura E. - John M. PLATT
STRICKLAND, Mary A. -
     Andrew C. HERRIFORD
STROUP, Mary Jane - James SHOBE
SULLIVAN, Mildred - Andrew MAXFIELD
SUTLIFF, Mary M. - Wm. R. VANOVER
SUTTON, America - Jessemon MELLON
   Mary Ann - Lorenzo RUNNELS
SWINNEY, Ann Eliza - Joshua EMBREE
SWITZLER, Caroline - Jos. TINDLE
   Lucy Ann - Benj. SMITH
SWOYER, Mrs. Maria - Josiah HODGE

TAPLEY, Louisa - John Wm. McCUNE
TAYLOR, Caroline - Robert
    HUSTON or HUESTON
   Mary S. - David MORRIS
   Elizabeth Jane -
    Appolinarius TUCKER
TATE, Mary F. - Preston B. REED
TERRELL, Almanda - Elias W. BARBEE
   Margaret M. - Wm. McCORMICK
THOMAS, Elizabeth - George KING
   Mrs. Malinda E. -
     George A. JOHNSON
   Susan - W. RICE
THORP, Susan - Joseph McCOY
THRUSTON, Sarah Washington -
    Dr. William THRUSTON
THURMAN, Rhoda Ann - Charles WRIGHT
   Susan M. - Samuel RHODES
TILDEN, Mary Jane - Z. C. ROBBINS
TITUS, Arethusa - Murdock MARTIN
TOOLEY, Mary Jane - Thomas J. HARVEY
TOLSON, Sarah - Enoch CREWS
TREADWAY, Mary - Col. A. RIDDLE
TRIGG, Diana - Maj. Shubael ALLEN
TRIMBLE, Margaret -
    John S. BROADWATER
TURNER, Ellen - John B. CLARK
   Elizabeth -Dr. J.C. PARRISH
   Jane - Benjamin CAVE
   Mary Ann - William WOODS
   Tabitha Ann - A. F. SETTLE
TYLER, Charlott - Benjamin JOHNSTON

ULRICI, Anna - G. William DREYER
   Clara - John WOLFF

VANDIVER, Joyce B. -
    Peter LA BEAUME
VANNOY, Margaret Ann -
    James RUTHERFORD
VENABLE, Amelia - A.J. ADERTON
VOGT, Mrs. Augusta -
    John J. KUMBERT

WALEY, Jane - Solomon FUNK
WALKER, Anna - Thomas SHORE
   Hellen -Dr. Alfred BASYE
   Mary Amanda -
    Jacob ELLISON
WALKUP, Margaret -
    Philip PRATHER
WALLACE, Lucy J. -
    Dr. James B. THOMAS
WALTON, Clarissa - Joseph SHANDS
   Elizabeth M. -
    James M. BULLARD
   Mary - George D. SHAW
   Nancy -
    Dr. James M. MARTIN
WARD, Ann - Dr. I. P. VAUGHN
WARDER, Mrs. Abigal -
    Caleb BELLES
WALSH, Mary Ellen -
    John HUMPHREYS
WASH, Mildred D. - Samuel LEWIS
WATERS, Fanny - Alfred P. ELLIS
WATSON, Ann Eliza -W.L. HICKMAN
   Emily - James HOUSEMAN
WATTS, Mrs. Sarah M. -
    George B. MURRAY
WEILS or Mrs. Jemima -
WELLS   John McDOWELL
WELLS, Fanny - S. F. MURRAY
WETHERILL, Ann L. -
    Theodore POINDEXTER
WHITE, Dorcas - John A. PAXTON
   Isabella - Robert WHITE
WHITEHILL, Mary J. - C. DuBOIS
WHITTLESEY, Mary Ann Augusta -
    Albert FAY
WILBURNE, Mrs. Mary -
    John MORTON
WILCOX, Mrs. Mary -
    Samuel PRIESTLY
   Sarah - James A. HILL
WILKINSON, Mary M. - John DARBY
   Serilda Ann -
    James A. JENKINS

WILLIAMS, Ann W. -
            Dr. William Henry HOARD
            Emily - Christo WHALLEY
            Frances A. -
                Capt. John CARLISLE
            Harriet A. - Edward PIKE
            Huldah E. -
                Dr. George W. HOOVER
            Mrs. Louisa- John STAPLES
            Malinda - Wm. B. NAPTON
            Maria - John W. HENRY
            Martha Ann - Henry M. BROWN
WILLIAMSON, Nancy M. - Wm. NORTH
            Sarah - Daniel SELTZER
WILLINGHAM, Lucinda -
            Barton Frances POWELL
WILLIS, Amanda C. - John DeGARIS
        Julia A. - James D. WOODS
WILLOCK, Virginia J. -
            Benjamin WALLACE
WILSON, Agnes - James HOWARD
        Mary - Samuel B. WIGGINS
        Mrs. Zarilda G. - Edward
            McAFEE or MACKFEE
WINLOCK, Magdalen - John STIRMAN
WINN, Dicey - Samuel L. B. PARKS
WINSTON, Louisa - Thomas P. MILLER
WISE, Lavinia - Henry J. WISE

WOLFSKILL, Margaret -
            Henry S. FOSTER
WOODS, Frances J. - Edw. GRAVES
        Martha J. - John SAMPSON
        Mary G. - Caleb STONE Sr.
WOODSON, Susan A. -
            Lieut. James H. MOSS
WOOLFOLK, Mary J. -
            William Henry BLOCK
        Rebecca A. -
            Francis CAKE
WOOLFORK, Mary M. -
            Capt. W. W. BAKER
WRIGHT, Mrs. Alta R. - Wm. EWING
        Catherine A. -
            Maj. Alexander MARTIN
        Frances -
            Samuel Green BALEY
WUNDERLICH, Susan -
            Alexander OLIVER

YOUNG, Eliza - James STONE
        Mary - Charles E. LORING
        Sally - Edward JOHNSON
        Sarah E. -
            Benjamin L. QUARLES

ZIMMERMAN, Zuliema A. -
            Dr. Wm. C. DUNCAN